MODERNITY AND AUTHENTICITY

SUNY Series in Social and Political Thought
Kenneth Baynes, Editor

MODERNITY AND AUTHENTICITY

A Study in the Social and Ethical Thought of Jean-Jacques Rousseau

ALESSANDRO FERRARA

STATE UNIVERSITY OF NEW YORK PRESS

Published by
State University of New York Press, Albany

For information, address State University of New York
Press, State University Plaza, Albany, NY 12246

Production by Christine M. Lynch
Marketing by Dana E. Yanulavich

Library of Congress Cataloging-in-Publication Data

Ferrara, Alessandro, 1953–.
[Modernità e autenticità. English]
Modernity and authenticity : a study in the social and ethical
thought of Jean-Jacques Rousseau / Alessandro Ferrara.
p. cm. — (SUNY series in social and political thought)
Translation of: Modernità e autenticità.
Includes bibliographical references.
ISBN 0–7914–1235–0 (acid-free). — ISBN 0–7914–1236–9 (pbk. : acid-
free)
1. Rousseau, Jean-Jacques, 1712–1778. 2. Authenticity
(Philosophy)—History—18th century. 3. Civilization, Modern—18th
century—Moral and ethical aspects. 4. Civilization, Modern—20th
century—Moral and ethical aspects. 5. Ethics, Modern. I. Title.
II. Series.
B2138.E8F4713 1993
170'.92—dc20
91–42018
CIP

10 9 8 7 6 5 4 3 2 1

For Antonio Guccione Monroy

CONTENTS

PREFACE

This work, completed in 1983 and first published in Italian in 1989, has a twofold structure. It is a study of the social and ethical thought of Rousseau in which the interpretive frame of reference used for reconstructing the unity of Rousseau's *oeuvre* is elucidated. But it is also a book on contemporary culture in which certain tendencies of today's culture are investigated through *Denkfiguren* typical of Rousseauian social theory. Of course, these two perspectives are always intertwined. Anyone who tries to reconstruct the thought of an author of the past does so with some question about the present in mind. On the other hand, it is impossible to reflect on the present without looking at it from some perspective anchored in the past. Usually, these two sides of interpretation are assigned a background and a foreground status. When the significance of the present is the primary focus, then we have a *Zeitdiagnose* or an essay in *culture criticism*. When instead some aspect of a past tradition is in the foreground, then we have a reconstruction in the history of ideas or a piece of philological analysis. Interpretive works differ, however, not only in terms of whether they seek to illuminate the past on the basis of the present or the

present on the basis of some past tradition, but also in terms of
the distribution of attention across the foreground and the
background. In "high contrast" works the perspective from
which the interpretation is carried out remains *implicit*, in "low
contrast" works the presuppositions of interpretation are made
explicit to a larger degree. Clearly, this book belongs in the second category.

I developed an interest in Rousseau by reading the sociological literature on contemporary culture and the transformation of the dominant personality structure in the advanced
industrial societies. I was struck by the conservative implications of positions such as those put forward by David Riesman,
Philip Rieff, Daniel Bell, Christopher Lasch and Richard Sennett. Although often motivated by critical intentions, these
authors seemed affected by the same inability, typical of all
conservativism, to point to anything positive in the present
beyond the perpetuation of the past. More recently the conservative thrust of all these positions, including those advocated
by the authors who intellectually came from the most progressive background, has fully revealed itself, for example in the
intellectual trajectory that has led Lasch from *The Culture of
Narcissism* to *The True and Only Heaven*. Be that as it may, the
hunch that the themes of *self-realization, authenticity* and *intimacy*, understood by the neoconservatives as the quintessential
marks of the present climate, could have been in fact more continuous with the tradition of Western rationalism than these
authors suspected led me to a revisitation of Rousseau's social
and ethical thought. I found interesting not only the similarity
between the main themes of Rousseau's work and the cultural
traits to which the neoconservatives call our attention, but also
the fact that the theme of authenticity was played by Rousseau
not in an *aesthetic* key, but rather in an *ethical* one, as the central
moment of a nonconservative critique of modernity.

At the same time, this essay on the ethic of authenticity
implicit in Rousseau was part of a larger attempt to reconstruct
the main turning points of the evolution of modern ethics from
the standpoint of the rationalization of culture. In a seminar
given at the University of California at Berkeley in 1980, Jürgen
Habermas discussed Weber's concept of cultural rationalization
in relation to the genesis of modern culture. Influenced by

Habermas's interpretation of Weber, later incorporated in his *Theory of Communicative Action*, I became interested in the possibility of applying the approach followed by Weber in his analysis of the significance of Puritanism for the evolution of Western culture to the *contemporary* developments of our ethical culture. More than answers, I borrowed from Weber a certain way of raising questions about the present. I wondered whether the contemporary tendencies discussed by the neoconservatives—and especially the generalized emphasis on self-fulfilment and self-realization—could be understood as responses, belated and still incomplete, to *new* cultural tensions, typical not so much of the transition to a modern culture—e.g. the tensions investigated by Weber—as of the transition to a qualitatively distinct stage of modernity.

From this perspective the project of assessing the coherence, complexity and internal balance of the responses developed by various authors and traditions to the new tensions of modern morality began to take shape. And an unsuspected relevance of Rousseau's ethical thought began to emerge. However, the attempt to reconstruct the *tradition of authenticity* (Rousseau, Schiller, Kierkegaard, Nietzsche, Heidegger) as a moral vocabulary competing with the more influential *tradition of autonomy* (Kant, Hegel, the Utilitarians, up to Habermas and Rawls) and to point out its elective affinity with our contemporary response to the new cultural tensions of modernity has gradually been modified, during the past few years, up to the point of legitimating the use of the past tense when referring to it. This project has been replaced, at the center of my research interests, by the attempt, less historical and more systematical, to articulate in a theory of judgment or *phronesis* that mode of argumentation and justification, based on the notion of identity, which is implicit in every ethic of authenticity and at the same time constitutes one of the distinctive traits of our contemporary sensibility.

This book could not have been written without the influence of several teachers and the generosity of a number of institutions. Among the institutions, I wish to thank the University of California for two University Fellowships which allowed me, during the years 1980–81 and 1981–82, to work intensively on my Ph.D. dissertation at the Department of Sociology at Berkeley, and the Alexander von Humboldt Foundation, which supported my research at the Max Planck Institut of Munich and at the Department of Philosophy of the University of Frankfurt during the years 1982–83 and 1983–84. Among the teachers, I am very grateful to Neil J. Smelser, who supervised the dissertation on which this book was originally based and offered continuous suggestions and encouragement, and to Jürgen Habermas, whose invaluable criticism forced me to revise my argument in many points and to spell out further my concept of authenticity. Also, the development of my thoughts has been influenced in important ways by several discussions with Kenneth Bock, Randy Baker, Chuck Stephen, Andrea La Porta, Walter Privitera, the members of the Colloquium at the Department of Philosophy of the University of Frankfurt, and my colleagues in the Workshop on Modernity at the Department of Sociology of the University of Rome.

Very special thanks are due to Donatella Caponetti, for having shared with me all the aspects of the production of this text: theoretical, editorial and, last but not least, emotional. Finally, I wish to thank my first teacher of philosophy, Antonio Guccione Monroy for having taught me, during the years of my university studies in Palermo, more than he might suspect. To his memory this first book of mine is gratefully dedicated.

Rome, September 1991.   *Alessandro Ferrara*

INTRODUCTION

Today, Rousseau is read less than he deserves and, when he is read, usually his image and significance are flattened to just one aspect of his life-work. There exists a Rousseau political theorist—the author of *The Social Contract*, of the two Discourses and few other works—mostly ignored by those who are familiar with the author of the *Reveries*, of *The New Heloise*, and of the *Dialogues*. Then there is a Rousseau pedagogist, confined to *Emile* and little known to either of the preceding kinds of readers. Underlying the various aspects of Rousseau's work, however, a thematic coherence can be detected. In the present essay I will try to highlight this coherence by reconstructing Rousseau's critique of Western modernity and his implicit ethic of authenticity. My intent, however, is not merely of a philological nature. Rather, I was attracted to Rousseau by a certain affinity between the central themes of his work, especially his conception of ethics, and some of the cultural tendencies that

1

since a few decades have begun to pervade the moral climate of the advanced industrial societies. Thus, another aim of this book is to bring out the sense in which Rousseau's work retains some relevance for the discussion of a number of contemporary issues.

Over the past few years, the terms "postmodern" and "postmodernity" have gained a wide currency within American and European social theory as labels for designating a cultural situation which is perceived as distinct from the modernity of the last three centuries. At first sight, these expressions might seem paradoxical. For, according to any dictionary, the terms "modern" and "modernity" merely identify the temporal position of a form of consciousness or of any cultural product relative to those which have preceded it in history. However, the modern age is so closely identified with the rise of the economic, political and social order inspired by bourgeois culture, that it has become possible to make sense of such terms.[1] From a substantive point of view, I take for granted that it makes sense to see our contemporary period as different in important ways from what has thus far been called modernity and should perhaps be renamed *early* modernity. What this difference consists of and how it can be best characterized are questions which still await an answer.

Let me delimit the problem in a more precise way. Modernity is a complex phenomenon which has unfolded in the distinct domains of social institutions, culture and personality. We can speak of an *economic-political* modernity, defined by the rise of the market economy, the nation-state and bureaucratic organizations, and by the industrial revolution. We can speak of a *cultural* modernity, distinguished by the differentiation of the religious-metaphysical world-view of the Middle Ages into specialized and increasingly institutionalized spheres of meaning. These spheres of meaning are regulated by standards of validity which remain logically independent of one another— i.e., the standard of truth and utility in the sphere of cognition and instrumental action, the standard of justice and the good life in the domain of morality and social interaction, the standard of beauty and authenticity in the realm of artistic and, more generally, self-expressive activities. Finally, we can speak of the rise of a *modern type of personality*, characterized through the orientation to reason rather than the authority of tradition, through a greater capacity for self-direction, and through the emphasis on a rational conduct of life.

For each of these three aspects of modernity we can point to important historical changes which set our contemporary predicament in a special position. As far as the economic and political aspects of modernity are concerned, we can point to the increased intervention of the state into the economic process, to the creation of welfare institutions aimed at redressing the undesirable effects of the accumulation and concentration of capital, to the rising role of the tertiary sector in all the advanced economies, to the softening of the conflict of labor and capital, to the increasing incorporation of technology and science (natural in the first place, economic and social in the second) within productive and administrative activities and, finally, we can point to the shift from production geared to existing needs to the artificial inducement of new needs as a way of expanding production.

As for the cultural aspects of modernity, we can point to the divorce of art and realistic representation which occurred at the turn of the century, to a reawakening of interest in the sphere of the sacred, to a diffused sense that the modern spirit of differentiation has now gone too far in the way of separating the culture of experts and everyday culture and, finally, to an increasing concern for the damage inflicted by our social practices on nature, both internal and external.

As for the sphere of personality in our times, we can point to the shift of basic pathologies from a predominance of neurotic traits linked with anal-retentive character configurations to a predominance of borderline disturbances linked with oral and narcissistic character configurations, and we can also point to an increasing flexibility in adapting to change as well as to an increasing gregariousness. This latter feature has been emphasized by an impressive number of authors, from the early critics of mass society to the founding fathers of the Frankfurt School, and up to the neoconservative critics of today's culture. Ortega y Gasset, Herbert Marcuse, Theodor W. Adorno, Daniel Bell, Erich Fromm and David Riesman have each advanced the claim that the fragile turn towards autonomy which occurred during early modernity is now giving way to a renewed heteronomy. The heteronomy of this new form of life, however, is no longer oriented toward tradition but rather toward the peer-group and the mass-media.

Rousseau's work can contribute little to the understanding of changes in the economic and political aspects of modernity and only very indirectly to the understanding of the transformations that have affected the sphere of personality. However, a reconstruction of his social theory and ethics can help us to see under a different light the transformations under way at the level of *cultural* modernity. Again, in order to grasp the contemporary relevance of Rousseau's thought we will have to focus on a specific area within the broad boundaries of what pertains to cultural modernity. I will neglect the important contributions given to the individuality of our epoch by the unprecedented accumulation of scientific knowledge, by the incorporation of science within the forces of production or by the diffusion of aesthetic modernism. Instead, I will concentrate on some changes that have occurred in the *moral sphere* and on their repercussions for the individual and for the social order. Within the sphere of morality, I will pay less attention to the effects of social-structural processes upon the evolution of ethical thought and more to the inner logic of its evolution. Changes at this level—as it is shown by Weber's analysis of the role of the Protestant ethic in the emergence of modern society— are among the ones which carry the broadest implications for the survival or the demise of an institutional order. Yet changes of this sort are among the most elusive and difficult to grasp conceptually. Ingrained as they are in the texture of everyday life, the changes located at the interface between culture and personality, between moral life and identity, are very much part of the common experience of people. Although they are perceived by everybody, these changes are often misinterpreted and attributed to the changing "psychology" of others. Momentous transformations of social relations and institutions are then reduced to sudden and inexplicable modifications of the "character" of people or to the willful subversion of the ways of tradition. As is usually the case with the phenomena which really mark an epoch, there hardly exists a theory-neutral language in which to describe the cultural transformations which affect the contemporary climate of Western societies. In the next chapter I will briefly summarize the account of these transformations provided by a number of leading culture critics, then I will comment on their analyses and finally I will outline the relevance of Rousseau's work to this discussion.

1

CONTEMPORARY MODERNITY
AND ITS DISCONTENTS

Among American social theorists, and to some extent in Europe as well, a strand of culture criticism has become influential, which rightly insists on the distinctiveness of contemporary modernity but tries to capture this distinctiveness in terms of an apocalyptic pessimism. Authors of diverse inspiration and interested in different aspects of today's culture such as Daniel Bell, David Riesman, Richard Sennett, Philip Rieff and Christopher Lasch, all converge on the main lines of a neoconservative *Zeitdiagnose*. The suggestive expressions often used by them— "the triumph of the therapeutic," "the fall of public man," "the culture of narcissism," "post-ascetic culture"—point to a more or less integrated complex of symptoms. The "postmodern" syndrome can at bottom be characterized as an endemic uneasiness with the rationalistic bent of Western culture. According to this perspective, normative ideas such as the ideas of duty, reason or morality have become, along with all universalistic claims, inherently suspicious. Both in the products of high culture and in the popular consciousness, the emphasis is rapidly shifting from the rational, the planned, the instrumental, the universal and the normative to the spontaneous, the playful, the emotional, the immediate and the unique. More specifically, in the moral life an ethos is taking a firm hold, which again can be best characterized by its stress on feeling and immediacy, its disavowal of responsibility, its cynicism, its exceedingly tolerant relativism and, above all, by its tendency to distort ethical categories into the metaphors of sickness and health. A major shift is also affecting that area, a sensitive one for all modern morality, which consists of our intuitive image of the good life. In this area the transformations under way are gradually undermining, according to this view, the traditional Puritan equation of self-realization and success in the sphere of work. This Puritan view is in the process of being rapidly replaced by the equation of self-realization and consumption in the fifties and early sixties, and of self-realization and personal growth in the seventies and eighties—where personal growth means the acquisition of a deeper and deeper awareness of the self and capacity for entering genuinely intimate relationships. The syndrome includes also the devaluation of public life and an increasing disaffection with routine politics. In the words of Richard Sennett, to which all of the above mentioned authors would subscribe,

> the reigning belief today is that closeness between persons is
> a moral good. The reigning aspiration today is that the evils
> of society can all be understood as the evils of impersonality,
> alienation and coldness. The sum of these three is an ideology
> of intimacy: Social relations of all kind are real, believable and
> authentic the closer they approach the inner psychological
> concerns of each person.[1]

As regards the sphere of personality, all these authors express alarm at the alleged decline of autonomy. Their terminologies may differ, but again "the other-directed character," "the narcissistic personality," "psychological man" and other expressions of the kind point to a common core of psychological features. Among these features we find: a quality of self-absorption and egocentrism, unbridled cravings for recognition and possession disguised by a superficial show of 'togetherness', a dependence on external approval for a sense of self-worth, and a weakening of internalized moral controls. Alongside the weakness of the superego the single element on which the widest convergence can be noticed is the transition from *guilt* to *anxiety* as the prevailing modality of self-control. Contemporary man is growing more and more impervious to the pangs of conscience but more and more frightened to lose the reassuring smile of others. Finally, the "postmodern" syndrome is evaluated in extremely negative terms. The neoconservatives view our time as marked by a "loss of rationality," i.e. by a sudden and radical departure from that rationalist emphasis of Western culture which less than a hundred years ago was proclaimed by Max Weber to lie on a line of development of "universal significance and value."[2] Furthermore, today's trends are believed to prelude to the disappearance of the Western form of individuality and to a return to frightful forms of barbarism and incivility.[3]

Let me briefly examine the way in which such themes are developed by each of these authors. D. Bell ascribes the rise of the postmodern syndrome to the diverging principles underlying the economic order and contemporary culture. According to him, today's culture is no longer capable of inducing and stabilizing the motivations functional to the maintenance of the social system. The economic and productive structure of society continues to be pervaded by the value of *efficiency*, whereas the culture has ceased to stress restraint and industriousness and has started to emphasize the immediate gratification of desire and self-realization. Instead of setting a norm against which to assess the new and, if necessary, reject it, contemporary culture for Bell puts an absolute value on the new and the search for novel forms of experience.[4] Behind the products of our culture Bell sees a "megalomania of self-infinitization" which consists in the refusal to accept limits, in the idea that nothing is forbidden and all is to be explored, and in the search for a destiny that is always beyond—beyond good and evil, beyond tragedy, beyond culture itself.[5]

How did such predicament come about? Since the mid-nineteenth century, argues Bell, a new notion of the self has arisen and has produced important changes in our world-view. What is unique to each individual is now considered the highest good and the enhancement of this uniqueness has become the ultimate value. Writes Bell,

> In Western consciousness there has always been tension between the rational and the non-rational, between reason and will, between reason and instinct, as the driving forces of man. Whatever the specific distinctions, rational judgment was traditionally thought to be superior in the hierarchy, and this order dominated Western culture for almost two millennia. Modernism dirempts this hierarchy. It is the triumph of the spirited, of the will.[6]

As a result of the rise of this ideology, rooted in *aesthetic modernism*, morality and all that is normative have come under attack. What matters now, in our judgment of conduct, is the impact of the action on the self and not the moral consequences to society.[7] The origin of such contemporary myths as the ideal of the "untrammeled self" or of living one's life as a work of art is to be found, according to Bell, in the ideal of the total autonomy of artistic activity from both sponsors and conventions. According to this ideal, which had its foremost spokesman in Baudelaire, artistic creation is the conscious and willful transgression—on the part of an imprisoned subjectivity—of the constraints set by society and by tradition. The innovative results of these acts of transgression subsequently crystallize into new models and standards which again must be broken through. The current climate would then be the product of the trickling down of the "idolatry of the self" from the exclusive milieus of the avant-garde to popular culture. According to Bell, this process of diffusion, under way for a century, was favored by two factors. On one hand, the formerly "functional" orientations embedded in the Protestant ethic gradually lost their functionality.[8] On the other hand, the opportunities for the "adversary culture" to gain influence have multiplied. The expansion of the culture industry, with its publishing houses, art galleries, newspapers, weeklies and monthlies, museums, theaters, movie studios, radio and television stations, etc. has quantitatively increased the size of the cultural elite. The modernistic elite has grown from a bohemian enclave to a powerful group bound by a consciousness of kind, and to the extent that this class increases its influence upon society so do its ideas.[9] Consequently, the motivations necessary for the functioning of the market, for the division of labor and for the political process are chronically in short supply. The problem then becomes, for Bell, how to find a functional equivalent of the declining work ethic, i.e. some cultural code capable of relegitimating attitudes of restraint and industriousness. Only a religious revival, concludes Bell, can return the contemporary individual "to the existential predicaments which are the ground of humility and care for others."[10]

The destabilizing effect attributed by Bell to aesthetic modernism is imputed by other authors—especially by Rieff and by Lasch—primarily to what they call "the therapeutic mentality." This mentality, which they see as originating in the ethical nihilism of Freud's psychoanalysis, is supposed to have gained an increasing influence on the whole society through the diffusion of therapeutic practices. According to this second version of the neoconservative *Zeitdiagnose*, exposure to psychotherapy rather than to aesthetic ideologies of self-realization is the variable which can explain the increasing diffusion of antirationalist outlooks. David Riesman's work, which precedes Lasch's and Sennett's endeavors by about twenty-five years, belongs in this second variety of neoconservatism. Character-change is at the center of his famous work of the fifties, *The Lonely Crowd*.[11] For Riesman, modernization has meant, at the level of the personality, a general transition from a type of character oriented to tradition to an inner-directed individual, capable of positing autonomous goals and standards and of taking, if needed, a critical stance vis-à-vis the orientations of the community. Today, Riesman denounces a new shift from the greater autonomy of the inner-directed character to a renewed form of heteronomy, which he calls "other-directedness." The other-directed individual is as little capable of distancing himself from external models as was the tradition-directed type. The difference is that instead of orienting themselves toward the immutable patterns of the past, present-day individuals set their "inner gyroscope" by the ever-changing moods of their contemporaries, either those personally known to them or those with whom they come in contact through friends or the mass media.[12] Riesman explains the shift on the basis of the changing patterns of child-rearing which, in turn, are largely determined by the state of flux of certain basic value-orientations. He contends that the loss of old certainties in the sphere of work and social relationships causes parents to become uncertain about the proper way to raise children. Uncertainty, in turn, leads parents to seek expert advice and to become very receptive to the influence of the mass media. Today's parents "cannot help but show their children, by their own anxiety, how little they depend on themselves and how much on others."[13] Regardless of the content of their teach-ings, anxious parents continuously convey the message that the approval of others, be they school-mates or teachers, peers or the boss, is the only unequivocal good to which one can orient one's conduct: "One makes good when one is approved of." Consequently, the child "learns from his parents' reactions to him that nothing in his character, no possession he owns, no inheritance of name or talent, no work he has done is valued for itself but only for its effects on others."[14] Riesman stresses, as subsequent work on narcissism and socialization confirmed, that anxious parents cannot but breed anxious children.[15] The effects of the parents' uncertainties are compounded by the influence of teachers who find themselves in an analogous predicament. Although they are assigned a greater responsibili-ty than their predecessors (for example, they are told that "bad behavior" on the part of the children ultimately implies "bad management" on their part), they have less means available for controlling the child than in the past when stern discipline was the norm. As a result, teachers also tend to become anxious, to feel dependent on the children's approval and to convey to them the implicit request that they "be nice," thus indirectly reconfirming the notion that "to be uncooperative is about the worst thing one can be."[16] The portrait of the other-directed indi-vidual drawn by Riesman is quite in line with all the elements of the postmodern syndrome. Controlled through manipulation during his or her childhood, the other-directed individual also controls others through manipulation, while craving intimacy and warmth nonetheless. He or she devalues public life and professes a cynical tolerance which only masks a lack of genuine interest in anything beyond the self. To the extent that he or she does take an interest in the public sphere, the other-oriented individual is less concerned with evaluating policies and decisions than with appraising leaders in terms of their personality and "sincerity." Socialized into feeling self-cohesion only as a reflection of the approval of others, the other-directed person vitally needs friends, whereas the tradition-oriented individual relied on the extended family and the inner directed character was more of a lone wolf. The more the other-directed person is denied fulfilment in work, the more self-realization in intimacy will appear crucial to him or her.[17] According to Riesman, these transformations are quite deleterious to the sphere of morality. The title of one of the chapters of *The Lonely Crowd* —"From Morality to Morale"—already suggests Riesman's conclusion. A socialization process which induces anxiety and reinforces self-doubt leaves few chances for the development of a genuine concern for the right. In fact, it undermines the character structures that enable individuals to stand against their group in defense of what they deem right. The concern for acting "rightly" gives way to a concern for group morale. In one of his most recent works, Riesman brings his analysis closer to the ideas of Bell, Sennett and Lasch. He describes the "truly dramatic change" of our times as a process that directly threatens the sphere of morality. Hypocrisy has now become, in his view, a worse vice than egocentricity.[18]

Philip Rieff's account of the culture of contemporary modernity shares with Riesman's an emphasis on personality change. The diremptive role played for Bell by the modernist consciousness is played for Rieff by the "therapeutic mentality." In Rieff's analysis the fortunes of psychotherapy are at the same time the fortunes of a newly emerging character type, "shrewd," "antiheroic," self-centered and who considers "unprofitable commitments as the sins most to be avoided."[19] This new character is *psychological man*. Although more proudly Nietzschean than Riesman's other-directed individual or Lasch's narcissistic personality, psychological man shares with these other fellow travelers of "postmodernity" a number of important traits, namely privatism, the retreat from politics, the aversion to commitments, a hedonistic longing for the satisfaction of each desire as well as a sour impatience with morality, which he assimilates to sheer repression. The only commitment, continues Rieff, to which we now thoroughly subscribe is the "gospel of self-fulfilment."[20] The prospect for morality is bleak. For the ultimate aim of today's "antipolitical revolution" is "the permanent disestablishment of any deeply internalized moral demands."[21] As Rieff puts it

> Our cultural revolution does not aim, like its predecessors, at victory for some rival commitment, but rather at a way of using all commitments, which amounts to loyalty towards none.... The wisdom of the next social order...would not reside in right doctrine, administered by the right men, who must be found, but rather in doctrines amounting to permission for each man to live an experimental life.[22]

The consequences of this predicament for politics are equally devastating. According to Rieff, when the transition to the therapeutic mentality will be completed,

> All governments will be just, so long as they secure that consoling plenitude of option in which modern satisfaction really consists.... Problems of democracy need no longer prove so difficult as they have been. Psychological man is likely to be indifferent to the ancient question of legitimate authority, of sharing in government, so long as the powers that be preserve social order and manage an economy of abundance.[23]

In the current triumph of the therapeutic mentality Rieff sees the coming true of the gloomiest among the alternatives outlined by Weber at the end of *The Protestant Ethic*. No way out of the iron cage is in sight and the advent of "new prophets," if possible at all, seems more remote by the day. Thus the problem which Rieff, as Bell, considers the most urgent—i.e., how to rehabilitate restraint—is destined in his view to remain unsolved for quite some time. In fact, Rieff shares neither Bell's hope for an imminent reawakening of religious feelings nor Weber's belief in its mere possibility.

In *The Fall of Public Man* Richard Sennett concerns himself with the erosion of public life and the growth of an ideology of intimacy which he considers typical of contemporary modernity.[24] In his analysis Sennett combines Tocqueville's theory of "soft despotism" with Weber's image of the "iron cage." Tocqueville saw the reason for the increasing privatization of society mainly in the growth of equality. Equality inclines the citizens to concentrate on their private fortunes and enterprises. Alongside their love for liberty, the citizens of an egalitarian democracy come then to share a desire to hand the burden of administrative decisions over to bodies of appointed specialists, i.e. politicians and bureaucrats. Soon they are reduced to an "innumerable multitude of men" indifferent to anything beyond their private pleasures. Each citizen becomes "almost unaware of the fate of the rest": "Mankind, for him, consists in his children and his personal friends." Consequently, the citizens of an egalitarian democracy become increasingly dependent on a political power to which they themselves have given the mandate to secure their enjoyment and watch over their fate. This power for Tocqueville will be "absolute, thoughtful of detail, orderly, provident and gentle." In the end the citizens of an egalitarian democracy do not lose their liberty, as in a tyranny, but do not retain it in its entirety either. Rather, they are trapped in a cycle in which they "quit their state of dependence just long enough to choose their masters and then fall back into it."[25] Sennett tries to merge this view of the tendencies of democracy with Weber's themes of the increasing rationalization of society and of the disenchantment of the modern world. Large bureaucracies promote a "protean" kind of skill, argues Sennett, i.e. the capacity to quickly reconvert one's abilities and to adapt to a new human environment. In this way, bureaucratization indirectly promotes a concern with the self and with personal relations over a concern with "things" or with objective performance. On the other hand, the decline of the idea of a realm of transcendent meanings also contributes to the subjectivization of society. These factors converge in producing the "fall of public man" and the rise of a culture of intimacy.

The clash between the two cultures—i.e. the culture of restraint and achievement of early modernity and the culture of selfexpression and gratification of contemporary society—is thus reformulated by Sennett as the clash between a culture of "civility" and the present-day culture of "self-absorption." The culture of civility was a culture of social distance and of politeness which flourished in the large cities of the eighteenth century—especially in Paris and London—and allowed people to interact sociably in the streets, in the pubs and in the clubs without ever bringing their private concerns into play.[26] In the context of that culture nothing negative was thought of the impersonality of public and, more specifically, of political roles. Citizens formed an attentive audience and were ready to take part in the political process. Our contemporary culture, instead, views impersonality as evil and considers intimacy "a moral good." According to this ideology of intimacy, continues Sennett, social relations are valued only to the extent that they reflect our private concerns and assuage our psychological needs. For Sennett the diffusion of these views erodes the basis, motivational and cultural, of any concern with political and communal interests. Two of the main phenomena which accompany the transition from the culture of civility to that of self-absorption are the resurgence of charismatic styles of leadership and what Sennett calls "destructive Gemeinschaft." Because of the shrinking of the public sphere, today people approach public matters not in terms of impersonal criteria but of their personal feelings. Typically, political leaders are considered "credible" in terms of what kind of a person they are, rather than in terms of the actions or programs that they espouse.[27] The term "destructive Gemeinschaft" designates an interest in the affairs of one's community which is based primarily on questions of identity. Instead of being concerned with substantial issues and with concrete results—by which Sennett means success in the arena of special interests politics—today people understand their involvement in collective action as directed at drawing a line between those who truly belong to the community and those who do not. In this way the delimitation and definition of collective identity—a sort of public analogue of the narcissistic preoccupation with self-image—becomes the all-encompassing issue, over and beyond the concrete needs and conflicts which motivate a community to collective action in the first place. The Dreyfus affair, the dispute over the Forest Hill community in New York and Nixon's Checkers Speech are for Sennett the best examples of the new incivility in our political life.

Four factors, according to Sennett, have played a special role in the occurrence of this major cultural transformation. One is the separation of the workplace from the household, which contributed to create the ideology of the family as an island of warmth in the cold impersonality of modern society. Urbanization, bureaucratization and secularization constitute the other three.[28] More specifically, among the effects of secularization Sennett considers the rise of a fear of the involuntary disclosure of self in public, which he takes to have motivated people to seek refuge in intimacy.[29] Of all the neoconservative critics of contemporary culture, Sennett is certainly the most outspoken in defending the old culture. He wishes to see the gap between public and private conduct restored in full force, he has a nostalgia (shared with Riesman and Rieff) for the "masks of sociability" of the urban culture of two centuries ago, he tends to understand politics as a competitive struggle for power, and he seems to suggest that a return to the ruthlessness and rapacity of the old possessive individualism is the only alternative to narcissism and the soft despotism.[30] In his interpretation contemporary modernity appears characterized once again as a *loss*. More precisely, it is described as a loss of distance in social relations which in turn affects one's relation to the self and to the things upon which judgment is passed. Without distance everything can only be appraised in terms of its suiting the self, not in its own merit. Underlying this vision is the idea that "because every self is in some measure a cabinet of horrors, civilized relations between selves can only proceed to the extent that nasty little secrets of desire, greed or envy are kept locked up."[31] As the old ones did, also the new conservatives such as Sennett remain silent as to why the "nasty little secrets" have become second nature to people.

Christopher Lasch's interpretation of contemporary culture is perhaps the most penetrating among those examined here, but also the most ambiguous. If one keeps close to his stated intentions it would be unfair to label him a neoconservative. Yet, even though Lasch is the social critic who most sees through the narrowness of the thesis of the decline of rationality, in the end he remains caught in it. Some of his statements in *The Culture of Narcissism* echo Rieff's theme of the "triumph of the therapeutic" and Bell's critique of the "adversary culture" without adding much. Lasch takes for granted that "selfabsorption defines the moral climate of contemporary society,"[32] and that the therapeutic mentality is bound to undermine morality.

Therapy labels as sickness what might otherwise be judged as weak or willful action; it thus equips the patient to fight (or resign himself to) the disease, instead of irrationally finding fault with himself. Inappropriately extended beyond the consulting room, however, therapeutic morality encourages a permanent suspension of the moral sense.[33]

Again, this predicament is linked with the perverse effects of a Freudianism which, "having displaced religion as the organizing framework of American culture," now threatens "to displace politics as well."[34] Narcissism, however, is not to be seen as a cultural pattern only. Lasch claims that the *prevailing character type* has already shifted towards a narcissistic direction. However, I will leave this argument aside. Even though Lasch goes at great lengths to show that his analysis is grounded on the recent psychoanalytic literature, especially on the work of Kohut and Kernberg,[35] he translates clinical claims into sociological ones in a rather mechanical way. Consequently, his account of the new emerging character differs very little from Riesman's except for the terminology. All the key variables are the same: the shrinking of the family in size and function, the absent father, the moral insecurity of the parents, their anxiety, their seeking advice from experts and the media, the indirect reinforcement of anxiety which accompanies the obtaining of expert advice, and the role of the peer-group as a socializing agency. The discrepancy between Lasch on one side and Bell, Sennett and Rieff on the other has to do with the angle from which Lasch criticizes the phenomena at hand. Yet this is also the point where the gap between his intentions and what he really does begins to open up. In his book he conducts a polemic against the facile criticism, halfway between journalism and self-confession, which described the seventies as the "Me" decade and neglected the *social* roots of cultural change. For the image of two cultures that tear society apart Lasch wants to substitute an image of continuity, albeit a continuity in decadence. The therapeutic mentality only presents itself as emancipation, self-infinitization and transgression. In fact, in opposition to Bell, for Lasch the therapeutic mentality is highly *functional* in a social life dominated by the large bureaucracies. To the extent that the individual becomes more dependent on impersonal organizations, argues Lasch, we should not be surprised to see the tendency toward self-absorption gain ground. For narcissism represents nothing but the psychological result of this social dependency.[36] In contrast to the demonization of cultural forces which characterizes much of the neoconservative critique of the contemporary ethos, Lasch must be credited for directing our attention, as Adorno and the tradition of Critical Theory have long insisted, on the fact that the glorification of privatism, self-fulfilment and intimacy is reaching its peak precisely when the possibility of true individuation seems to have receded most. According to Lasch, "it is the devastation of personal life, not the retreat into privatism, that needs to be criticized."[37] Unfortunately, this statement of intention is never fully carried out by Lasch. Most of *The Culture of Narcissism* and of the more recent study *The Minimal Self* contains culture criticism that can hardly be distinguished from the kind that Lasch wants to polemically attack, whereas only cursory comments are dedicated to the "social causes" of the devastation of personal life.[38] Finally, Lasch is unable to point to, from his own perspective, any element of today's culture which might count as a *progressive* distancing of the present moral climate from the culture of early modernity. For these two reasons Lasch's work can be assimilated to the neoconservative strand of cultural criticism.

This whole view of contemporary modernity has many more nuances that cannot be discussed in this brief review.[39] But why group these authors together under the common heading of neoconservatism? I believe that there are at least five distinct reasons for considering Bell and the others part of the same strand of social thought, the last two of which justify the neoconservative label. First, all these authors describe the cultural tendencies in question as recent or fairly recent developments. The beginnings of the new transformation go back from a maximum of a century (Sennett) to a minimum of three or four decades (Lasch, Rieff, Riesman). None of these authors ever considers the possibility that these developments could represent the belated unfolding of cultural tensions linked with the rise of modernity and, more specifically, of a modern morality.

Second, the cultural trends of industrial societies are described as a sudden and complete inversion of, or as a radical departure from, the direction of evolution so far followed by

Western culture—a thesis which the neoconservatives share with the enthusiastic supporters of "postmodernity" as a Dionysian liberation from modern rationalism. The positive emphasis on the break from Western modern rationalism as a distinctive achievement of contemporary modernity comes from many quarters. For example, we can find a similar emphasis in Feyerabend's methodological anarchism, in Derrida's critique of logocentrism, in Lyotard's critique of the modern "grand narratives" of progress and emancipation, in Rorty's denunciation of the search for "ultimate frameworks" and in his project for an ironic philosophy, in Foucault's defense of the material resilience and autonomy of the body againts the compulsion to self-control and self-discipline which forms the backcloth of the relation of the Western subject to its body, in Lacan's denunciation of the deceptive quality of any notion of a unitarian psychic subjectivity, and in Deleuze and Guattari's extolment of the irreducible primacy and plurality of desire.[40] Ironically, the neoconservative critics of the postmodern syndrome fall prey to the same cliché that they accuse the adversary culture of perpetuating. In fact, both the aesthetic modernists, the anti-modernist, antirationalist "postmodernists" and the conservative critics from opposite vantage points remain prisoners of the Nietzschean view of the "aesthetic" as inherently Dionysian and thus opposed to repressive individuation, to self-abnegation, to the rationalist quest for selfmastery, in sum as the Other or the antagonist of Reason. Both fail to realize that the aesthetic sphere, understood not only in the narrow sense of what pertains to art but also in the broader sense of what belongs to inner nature, constitutes not so much the realm of the irrational, as one of the moments of rationality along with the instrumental sphere and the ethical sphere and indeed contains, in the moment of the judgment of taste, the core of a nonrationalistic rationality or of a nongeneralizing universalism.

Third, for the authors reviewed above the cultural processes under way in contemporary society negatively affect the sphere of morality, but originate in other areas of culture or society, such as aesthetic ideologies or the economy or the family. None of them seriously examines the possibility that some of the elements in the postmodern syndrome—for example, the importance attributed to intimacy, self-realization and personal growth, or the impatience toward all ethical universalism disjoined from empathy and from a genuine appreciation for the uniqueness of each context of choice—may in fact derive from the autonomous evolution of the moral sphere. Through their approach the process of ethical rationalization which Weber reconstructed up to the rise of Protestantism appears to have come to a halt after the consolidation of a modern form of morality. The subsequent transformations of the Western ethos appear to have been caused exclusively by *external* factors, be they the fortunes of aesthetic outlooks or the vicissitudes of the family.

Fourth, none of these authors is capable of indicating any positive aspect in the cultural tendencies at issue. Bell, Rieff, Riesman, Lasch and Sennett approach the cultural climate of our time from an angle that blinds them to anything other than "decadence," because they look at the present in terms of its lacking some feature of the past, be it the culture of civility or the ethos of restraint, rather than as a constellation of meanings with positive features of its own. It is impossible to find in their writings the indication of any positive or progressive social change which has occurred after the 1930s. This inability is striking if compared with the epoch-marking grandiosity attributed to the transformations under way. Allusions to the slow rottening of the Roman Empire or to the rise of Christianity are not infrequent.[41] If one believes oneself to be faced with processes of this magnitude, is it not unreasonable to write off the tendencies under scrutiny as mere "decadence"? This one-sided moralistic analysis of our contemporary ethos as a deviation from the rationalistic bent of the Protestant ethic is just as simpleminded as it was, three centuries ago, to describe the Puritan ethos as a mere deviation from the old Catholic ethic of brotherliness—which in fact was the Counter Reformation's approach to the matter.

Fifth, each of the authors mentioned above is unable to propose any remedy for the ills of the postmodern syndrome other than the sheer restoration of the early-modern segment of social life which is at the center of his analysis. Sennett wishes to go back to the codes of social distance of the eighteenth century, to revive the masks of sociability and to rehabilitate the instrumental moment of politics. Rieff and Bell wish that some equivalent of the old ethic of sacrifice and self-abnegation be found. Lasch and Riesman wish to rescue the bourgeois family of the last century, which they assume to be the only agency capable of insuring an individuating form of socialization.

This last common trait provides in my opinion the strongest reason for grouping these authors together under the heading of neoconservatism. The prefix "neo," on the other hand, is justified by the novel attitude of this brand of conservatism towards modernity. Unlike the other indictments of the modern world voiced throughout the last two centuries, the indictment of today's culture expressed by the authors mentioned above does not amount to a monolithic rejection. None of these authors advocates a complete return to the past. Instead, they all presuppose a distinction between modernity as a political and economic phenomenon, i.e. democracy and the market economy, of which they approve, and modernity as cultural modernism, which to various degrees they all condemn because it endangers our chances to reap the fruits of the former.[42]

The more general reason why the perspective adopted by Bell, Rieff, Riesman, Lasch and Sennett leads them into a theoretical dead-end has to do with the unfortunate choice of Weber's pessimistic *Zeitdiagnose* as their starting point. The neoconservatives register the final divorce—anticipated in the Weberian metaphor of the "iron cage"—between the rational organization of production, politics and personal life typical of capitalism on the one hand, and the religious meanings that once legitimated such rationalization on the other. They observe the inability of our culture to produce any equivalent of an ethic orienting people toward restraint and self-abnegation. No "great rebirth of old ideas and ideals" seems imminent, no "new prophets" can be encountered, only individuals in search of self-fulfilment. Thus the neoconservatives end up merely repeating Weber's forecast. That is, the society which once found its ultimate frame of reference in the religious ideal of an orderly life devoted to the carrying out of one's calling is now split into the two opposing camps of the "specialists without spirit," devoted to work only as a means for securing consumption, and the "sensualists without heart," who dedicate their lives to aesthetic cultivation but remain insensitive to all sense of duty or communal purpose. The choice of this vantage point reveals its infecundity when the theorists of postmodernity combine it with Weber's dichotomy of *asceticism* and *mysticism*. When these two notions are superimposed over the distinction of specialists and sensualists we obtain, as a result, the gist of the neoconservative interpretation of contemporary modernity. Asceticism, which in a broader sense stands for *vita activa*, for a sense of moral purpose, for taking interest in the external world, for the desire to mold it, for self-transcendence, for believing in progress, for the desire to grow more in control of our collective destiny, and for the desire to free ourselves from all man-made yet unintentional constraints, is seen as losing ground. Mysticism, which is associated with *vita contemplativa*, with intellectualism without ethical commitment, with immobility and self-inspired stagnation, with withdrawal from the world and therefore with losing control over it, is seen as gaining the favor of the "sensualists without heart" and as threatening to become the dominant outlook. Because they mechanically transpose categories that once were useful for making sense of the early-modern world into their analysis of present-day culture, the neoconservatives miss what is perhaps most typical of our current climate. To the extent that the cultural processes under way in our societies can be captured with one formula, their sense appears linked not so much with inverting the early-modern way of ranking the instrumental and the aesthetic moments of rationality, or the ascetic and the mystical elements of our culture, as with *exploding* these dichotomies. The unsolved problem with which our culture is faced seems to be that of finding some way of compensating for the effects of the spirit of differentiation typical of early modernity and of healing the split between the cognitive and the aesthetic aspects, the intellectual and the emotional elements, the scientific and the religious moments of the Western form of life.[43]

The neoconservative interpretation of the cultural tendencies of the advanced industrial societies, however, contains an important insight. Some of the phenomena which have attracted the attention of Bell, Rieff, Sennett and the others do belong in the same picture. In spite of their diversity, phenomena as the diffusion of therapies, the decline of the ethic of work, the rise of a new equation of selfrealization and personal growth, the increasing disaffection with politics as a strategic confrontation between equally particularistic interests, the redistribution of character configurations from authoritarian to narcissistic modalities, the increasing emphasis on self-knowledge and autonomy from unrecognized inner urges, as well as the growing concern for the damages caused by the pressure of our social roles, add up to a complex of meanings in which we do recognize the stamp of our culture. More doubtful, however, is the idea that the common thread running through all these elements is an *aesthetic* ideology. It is more accurate to identify the underlying theme as the *moral* idea of the *authenticity of the person*—an idea which has slowly emerged during the last two hundred and fifty years but only recently has broken out of the boundaries of high culture. From the standpoint of cultural history, whereas early modernity can be characterized through the *idée-force* of *autonomy* from authority and from received opinion—an idea reasserted in science as in politics, in ethics as in aesthetics—contemporary modernity begins, at whichever point in history we locate the watershed, with the rise of the notion of *authenticity* to an equivalent role.

In philosophy the theme of authenticity has unfolded within a tradition of thought which has its origin precisely with Rousseau and which through Schiller and the early Romantics, through Kierkegaard, Nietzsche and Heidegger has come to influence contemporary culture. It is impossible for social theory to make full sense of the cultural trends of the advanced industrial societies without coming to terms with the way in which the work of these authors has contributed to shape our present ideas of a person, society, interaction, roles or identity. However, it would be misleading to regard the idea of authenticity as a legacy to be found exclusively in the teachings of these philosophers. In one form or another, sometimes intertwined with other themes, the notion of authenticity can be traced in almost all the important theorists of ethics and society of the last two centuries. Today a paradoxical development is under way. On one hand, the spokesmen of poststructuralism, deconstructionism and philosophical postmodernism who most explicitly refer to the teachings of Nietzsche and Heidegger—Foucault, Derrida, Lyotard, Rorty—avoid using the term authenticity because to their sensibilities it conveys the illusory myth of a totalizing, harmonious, unitary self, which they seek to replace with the image of a fragmented, plural, centerless and irreconcilably split subjectivity. Yet this image of the post-modern, centerless self is propounded in terms that imply that it carries a greater potential for authenticity than the early-modern image of the self-reflecting subject who is the master of its destiny. An authenticity *against* or *despite* the self or, in other words, a theme of authenticity played on the register of the *sublime* is here contrasted with the inauthenticity of the all-round notion of a *harmonious* authenticity. On the other hand, in certain developments of ethical and political theory we can see the rise of views of justice—such as those put forward by Walzer and Dworkin[44]—or of ethics centered on the notion of "progress for a tradition"—such as that developed by MacIntyre[45]—which arguably establish a systematic link between the notion of justice and the authenticity of a collective identity. It is impossible, however, to reconstruct the tradition of authenticity in its entirety or to trace out its transformations within the scope of this work. Instead, I will limit my focus to Rousseau, in that he is the initiator of the contemporary-modern reflection on the effects of the modern social order and the modern morality of autonomy upon the identity of the individual.

If we bring together the various aspects and themes of Rousseau's life-work—a life-work so fragmentary and antisystematic as to give rise to the partial and distorted images of "Rousseau the nostalgic of nature," "Rousseau the enemy of civilization," "Rousseau the totalitarian," "Rousseau the paranoid" and what not—it becomes apparent that a coherent idea underlies them. What gives unity to Rousseau's reflections on social reproduction, the just polity, education and ethics is, again, the notion of authenticity. Not only his way of posing these problems, but also the directions in which he looks for solutions as well as some of his substantive answers, anticipate to a surprising degree concerns and aspirations which only now have become the common stock of Western sensibility. Nowhere does Rousseau clarify the relation of his major works to one another, yet they form an organic whole in which the *Discourse on the Origin of Inequality* poses a problem and *The Social Contract*, *Emile* and *The New Heloise* represent three aspects of its solution. The problem which concerns Rousseau is the effect of social inequality and of competition upon the individual and social life. In the other three works Rousseau examines various aspects of an alternative form of social life, in which such effects are eliminated or at least mitigated. In *The Social Contract* he outlines a just political order, in *Emile* he investigates the conditions under which the growth of individual autonomy can be furthered, and in *Julie, or the New Heloise* we can find his implicit notion of a morality of authenticity. I will deal with these aspects of Rousseau's vision of an emancipated social life because they are the most prominent in his thought and are those on which his thought is most explicit.

In the next chapter I will be concerned with Rousseau's argument on society and the self. What remains most 'alive' in Rousseau's social criticism is not so much his attempt to have society emerge "naturally from nature," without man's disposition playing any role, but rather his twofold accusation against a social order based on competition. I will reconstruct the main steps of his account of the rise of a social order inimical to self-transparency and authenticity and will point to some internal difficulties.

In the third chapter I will be concerned with the alternative institutional order designed by Rousseau in *The Social Contract*. I will dwell on the social and motivational prerequisites for the formation of the general will, on Rousseau's procedural grounding of the legitimacy of the just polity and on his concept of freedom. At the same time, I will try to fit *The Social Contract* into the broader context of Rousseau's entire *oeuvre*. The public virtue on which the good functioning of the "social contract" depends cannot be generated "from above," by means of modifying the institutions only. Rather, a "private" virtue must be possessed to a certain extent by all the citizens in order for a society to move from a state of inequality to a just political order. This private virtue is linked with the acquisition of a moral conscience capable of judging on the basis of self-chosen principles and independent of the expectations of the community.

In the fourth chapter I will discuss Rousseau's ideas on how this quality of moral autonomy can be developed in the child, as they are expressed in *Emile*. I will try to specify Rousseau's notion of autonomy, to reconstruct the stages through which autonomy develops and to bring out the implicit psychological assumptions underlying his pedagogical views. In the end, however, the private virtue that can facilitate the transition to the order of the "social contract" is not exhausted by the notion of autonomy from the opinions and expectations of others. A number of other ingredients are indispensable. They can be grouped under the heading of *authenticity* and include empathy, selfknowledge, the capacity to accept the undesired aspects of the self, a sensitivity to the inner needs linked with the essential aspects of an identity, and a nonrepressive attitude towards one's inner nature. The acquisition of these aspects of private nature, however, falls beyond the scope of *Emile*, and Rousseau's ideas on the matter must be reconstructed from *The New Heloise*.

In the fifth chapter I will be concerned with Rousseau's novel. I will first review the plot of the novel and then will discuss its ethical implications. The implicit *ethic of authenticity* that can be found in Rousseau's novel—not as an articulate statement, but in the form of alternative courses of action that at some junctures of the plot the protagonist could have taken and later contrasts with the devastating consequences of her actual choice—completes the notion of that private virtue which Rousseau considers indispensable for the emancipation of social relations.

Finally, in the last two chapters, I will discuss the contemporary significance of Rousseau. On one hand, my reconstruction of Rousseau's social and ethical thought will be brought to bear on the neoconservative interpretation of today's cultural trends and, more specifically, on the hypothesis of a strong thematic link between the postmodern syndrome and aesthetic modernism. On the other hand, I will argue that Rousseau's work, when reconstructed along these lines, highlights the *ethical* roots of today's emphasis on authenticity, identity and self-realization, as well as the continuity of the theme of authenticity with the evolution of Western ethics.

More specifically, in chapter 6 I will contend that the relevance of Rousseau's implicit ethic of authenticity can be best understood with reference to the new cultural context and the new cultural tensions determined by the rise and affirmation of the Puritan ethos as the dominant ethos of the modern West. After clarifying, on the basis of a discussion of Weber, the sense in which we can speak of the evolution of ethics as process of *rationalization*, and after a cursory review of the main turning points of the development of Western ethics up to the rise of Protestantism, I will outline the new tensions created by the impact of the Puritan ethos in the sphere of morality.

This reconstruction provides then the background for a discussion, conducted in chapter 7, of the response offered by modern, secularized ethics to these modern tensions of morality. As Weber in "Religious Rejections of the World and their Directions" looked at Calvinism from the standpoint of its implicit response to the tension between the medieval ethos of brotherliness and the motivational requisites of the market and of the secular polity, it is possible to examine subsequent ethical conceptions from the standpoint of their implicit response to the new tensions generated by the Puritan ethos. Finally, I will argue that Rousseau's social and ethical thought contains the first *balanced* response that the Western tradition has offered to the new tensions of modern morality.

2

ROUSSEAU'S CRITIQUE OF MODERNITY

> Essentially, Rousseau did not wish
> for human beings to return to the
> state of nature. He rather meant
> that they should look back at it
> from the stage they are at now
>
> —Immanuel Kant[1]

Rousseau formulates his critique of modernity as a critique of
the effects of a social reproduction based on competition. This
critique, which constitutes the starting point for understanding
Rousseau's political theory, his views on education and his
implicit ethics, can be found mainly in the *Discourse on the Origin of Inequality*. Often taken as an abstract critique of society
and civilization in general, on closer inspection the "Second
Discourse" appears to be an argument against the principle of
social organization underlying modern Western society. The
societies and civilizations of the past are criticized by Rousseau
only insofar as they partake in a type of social reproduction
which Western modernity has developed to its extreme implications. Within this pattern of social reproduction participation in

the division of labor is rewarded through inherently divisive goods, such as wealth, power and prestige, which can function as incentives only to the extent that they are unequally distributed.

In spite of its brevity and its occasional character—it was meant as an entry for the essay contest called by the Academy of Dijon on the question "Which is the origin of inequality among men and whether it is allowed by Natural Law"— Rousseau's "Second Discourse" is a very dense and complex text. Rousseau starts out by drawing a portrait of human nature and of the life-conditions of presocial man, then proceeds to account for the rise of society and finally investigates the effects of this transition upon man. I will keep close to the sequential order of the various parts of the text. First I will reconstruct the explicit picture of human nature presented by Rousseau at the beginning. As the waters of a river are clear at the source, so is the image of man which opens up the "Second Discourse." However, as we follow Rousseau's argument downstream toward his conclusions, we encounter a number of points where the neatness of this image becomes quite muddled, due to the presence of conflicting argumentative goals. For example, in the context of his polemics against Hobbes, Rousseau is led to conceive of human nature as more limited and unintelligent than in the explicit picture. In his attempt to attribute the responsibility for human corruption to society Rousseau portrays man as much more distrustful. In the context of the explanation of the rise of society, however, man's nature is attributed a more rational quality than in the beginning of the Discourse. Finally, when Rousseau accounts for the transition from a patriarchal to the agricultural society man is implicitly portrayed as more prone to wickedness than in the "explicit picture." In the last section of the chapter I will reconstruct Rousseau's views on the effects of social life on human nature.

A. MAN IN THE STATE OF NATURE

The conceptual status of the state of nature has always been one of the controversial points in the literature on Rousseau. Did Rousseau intend to offer a historical and anthropological reconstruction of the beginnings of our species, or did he mean his description as a set of postulates, entirely speculative, that must be presupposed in order to make sense of the *present* state of man? Some commentators, usually the most unsympathetic to Rousseau, are inclined toward the first thesis, others toward the second; some interpreters suggest that Rousseau constantly wavered between the two alternatives; others that he set out for a hypothetical reconstruction but then, carried away by his own argument, ended up believing that his own axioms were a description of historical reality; and, finally, some contend that the fear of the reaction of the religious authorities of his time led Rousseau to disguise under the safe appearance of philosophical speculation what he actually believed to be a state-of-the-art scientific account of the origin of man.[2] Passages can be found that lend themselves to each interpretation, with one important difference. Namely, the passages that support the rationalist interpretation are usually literal and clear. Instead, the passages which support the realist reading do so only by virtue of their tone or of the intensity of feeling underlying the literal expression. This confers more weight to the hypothesis that Rousseau intended his description of the state of nature as a speculative endeavor. On the other hand, it is true that Rousseau appears to be very much concerned about the empirical plausibility of his assertions. He devotes long footnotes to the discussion of theories of the family, physical anthropology and travel memoirs. Yet this concern does not contradict his declared intent of undertaking "hypothetical and conditional reasonings" upon a state that after all may have never existed, but that nonetheless requires that we have "just notions" about it in order to "judge properly of our present state."[3] The fact that Rousseau tried to use the best knowledge available before formulating his hypotheses does not necessarily mean that he must have intended his whole argument as a factual account.

The innovative quality of the hypothetical and "counterfactual" argument developed by Rousseau in the "Second Discourse" was misunderstood for a long time. Marx, for example, certainly shared the critical intent of Rousseau, yet scorned all such attempts as "Robinsonades,"[4] forgetting that his own theoretical starting point, i.e. the idea of man as intrinsically social, was no less speculative than Rousseau's considerations on the state of nature. No theory of society can dispense with basic presuppositions, partly factual and partly speculative, which ultimately have to do with man's potentialities and propensities. Rousseau must be credited for having recognized this necessity, and also for having understood the futility of all attempts to lend more credibility to one's basic assumptions by presenting them as factual descriptions.

All theories of the state of nature share some common problems. The image of man that they presuppose must not include faculties which require the existence of society—thus for example Rousseau describes natural man as having no language, no desires beyond the immediate physical needs, no imagination, and no knowledge of the past or of the future. Yet, on the other hand, mankind must still be clearly distinguished from the other animal species. Rousseau's account of human nature is divided into a sort of physical anthropology, which we can neglect since it merely emphasizes the plausibility of imagining natural man well fit for the hardships of primitive life, and on the other hand a philosophical anthropology of the moral aspects of man. In his preface to the "Second Discourse" Rousseau characterizes human nature in terms of two basic drives: "one of them interests us deeply in our own preservation and welfare, the other inspires us with a natural aversion to seeing any other being, but especially any being like ourselves, suffer or perish."[5]

The first drive he calls "self-love," in opposition to "amour-propre," which instead is a thoroughly social product. The second drive is "pity." These two instincts, however, do not exhaust the distinctive qualities of human nature. Pity, for one thing, is not exclusively human. In fact, Rousseau makes pity so independent of reflection and self-consciousness "that the beasts themselves sometimes give evident signs of it."[6] Neither is self-love exclusively human. Hardly more complex than the instinct of self-preservation, self-love as described by Rousseau could be found in animals as well. In fact, following Descartes Rousseau describes animals as "ingenious machines" with built-in control mechanisms which "guard, to a certain degree, against every thing that might destroy or disorder" them. Furthermore, what makes man human is not the faculty of understanding either. For both man and the animals have sense-ideas and both combine these primary ideas into more complex ones.

The difference lies only in the various degree to which the animals and man are capable of abstraction.[7]

What is it, then, that sets man apart from the animals, if not his intelligence? *Free agency,* answers Rousseau. Whereas "nature alone operates in all the operations of the beast," man instead is a free agent and "has a share" in his own doings: "one chooses by instinct; the other by an act of liberty."[8] Rousseau adds then a second feature to his picture of human nature in order to better differentiate man from the animals. This new feature is the faculty of *self-perfection,* i.e. man's capacity to use his intelligence for the improvement of him self and of his living conditions. It has been rightly objected that a "faculty" of self-perfection is somehow tautological. The fact that as a species mankind has progressed to an extent unequaled by any animal species cannot be disputed and therefore, necessarily, there must have been a potential for such a development. Thus the faculty of self-perfection, understood as a potential for self-improvement inherent in the human being, would explain nothing.[9] Then the only quality, among those mentioned by Rousseau, which can set man apart from the animals is free agency or, rather, the consciousness of free agency.

Yet can the consciousness of free agency and of the self be entirely separated from social interaction? Here we reach the first juncture of the "Second Discourse" where the explicit picture of human nature drawn at the beginning undergoes deformation as a result of the pressure of a divergent argumentative goal. This pressure derives from Rousseau's polemic against Hobbes.

B. ROUSSEAU'S ARGUMENT AGAINST HOBBES

The difference between Rousseau's and Hobbes' notion of the state of nature concerns the struggle for existence and the passions that can be attributed to presocial man. Rousseau is willing to admit that over matters of immediate interest—such as one's share of a dead animal or the attention of a female—there could have been conflict in the state of nature. Yet since the passions involved supposedly never go beyond immediate needs, conflict is always limited and sporadic. Hobbes' argument to the effect that scarcity and the passions of man soon give rise to a war "where every man is Enemy to every man" is well known.[10] Rousseau's counterargument hinges on the distinction of 'self-love' and 'amour-propre.' Whereas the former exists in the state of nature, in order to conceive the rise of the war of all against all, and not simply of episodical outbursts of conflict, one needs to presuppose 'amour-propre'—i.e. men's capacity to see their own self and social standing as being attacked every time their possessions are attacked—and 'amour-propre' presupposes the existence of social life.[11] At this point Rousseau's argument runs into the first difficulty. For there seems to be no other reason, beyond its own definition, why 'amour-propre' cannot exist also in the state of nature. To the question "Why can men not compete with one another over the objects of their desire in the state of nature?" Rousseau answers that they cannot because they lack the motivations needed in order to sustain aggressive feelings past the immediate occasion for conflict. But to the next question, namely "Why can men not have these motivations?," Rousseau seems to answer in a circular way that they cannot because they are in the state of nature. To avoid begging the question Rousseau should provide an argument for why 'amour-propre' cannot exist in the state of nature which is not logically linked with the definition of the state of nature itself. This he does in the Note "o" of the "Discourse," where he contends that the feeling of 'amour-propre' rests on the ability to compare one's social standing to that of others and that natural man is in no position to make such comparisons. Rousseau maintains that

> selfishness does not exist in our primitive state, in the true state of nature; for every man in particular considering himself as the only spectator who observes him, as the only being in the universe who takes an interest in him, as the only judge of his own merit, it is impossible that a sentiment arising from comparisons, which he is not in a position to make, should spring up in his mind. For the same reason, such a man must be a stranger to hatred and spite, passions which only the opinion of having received some affront can excite; and as it is contempt or an intention to injure, and not the injury itself that constitutes an affront, men who don't know how to set a value upon themselves, or compare themselves one with another, may do each other a great deal of mischief,

as often as they can expect an advantage by doing it, without ever offending each other.[12]

To sum up, Rousseau's argument against Hobbes includes the following claims:

1. The Hobbesian state of a war of all against all requires such passions as hate, desire for revenge, greed, vanity and despise, which go beyond the contingencies of physical desire.

2. For these passions to go beyond the immediate occasion for conflict and be sustained over a long time it is necessary that they attach not so much to the object fought over as to the relative standing of the self of those concerned. This relative standing must be the real object of competition and conflict, of which the single objects under dispute are but the external symbols.

3. This ability to treat the outcome of singles episodes of conflict as something that affects one's relative standing requires the ability to draw comparisons between oneself and others.

4. In order to draw these comparisons one must be able to see oneself through the eyes of another, i.e. to distinguish one's self-perception from one's social image.

5. Natural man, however, is unable to make these comparisons, because he is thoroughly self sufficient, understands himself as "the only being in the universe which takes an interest in him," as "the only judge of his own merit," and regards the other members of his species under no "other light than he would animals of another species." Consequently, if he cannot make these comparisons, natural man cannot have the passions that can start and sustain the Hobbesian state of war. Furthermore, in the state of nature man has no idea of a future and thus a sentiment such as distrust, which Hobbes expected to induce men to try to anticipate future aggressions, could hardly arise. Even the fear of death, crucial in Hobbes'argument for men to see the necessity of a common pact, cannot be attributed to natural man any more than to animals.

However, even if rescued in this way from the accusation of circularity, Rousseau's argument gives rise to other difficulties. For example, how can the view of human nature embedded in his argument against Hobbes be reconciled with the quality of self-consciousness which Rousseau needs to postulate in order to set natural man apart from the animals? How is it possible for a man who hardly takes any notice of his fellow beings and who is totally independent of their help and opinion to develop a "consciousness of his freedom" and to take an interest in "judging himself"? Could we not apply Rousseau's critique of Hobbes to the "Second Discourse" and say that, just as Hobbes had projected on the state of nature passions which presuppose society, in the same way Rousseau attributes to natural man a consciousness of his acts and of his own being that necessarily presupposes the awareness of others? On the other hand, if natural man has enough cognitive capacities and self-consciousness to observe and judge his own conduct, why should he not be able to compare himself with others and compare his own with others' conduct? The tension between what Rousseau says explicitly about the state of nature and what he presupposes in his polemic against Hobbes is made even more strident by Rousseau's admission, in another context, that occasionally natural man does make comparisons. For instance, sometimes natural man is said to be able to weigh the worth of a prey against the risks of a fight and to evaluate the risks involved in dislodging somebody from his hut against the chances of finding another shelter or the toil of building a new one. Clearly, in order to carry out such comparisons one must already be able to compare one's own and others' capacities, one's own and others' willingness to take risks, and so forth.[13]

This tension can be eliminated if one realizes that Rousseau somehow overstated his point. As one critic has pointed out, Rousseau's position requires not that natural man should be incapable of making comparisons, "but that the comparisons he is in a position to make are made in a context in which each exists for himself alone as the only observing and judging consciousness in the world."[14] We can then rephrase Rousseau's argument and say that while in the state of nature men are indeed able to compare themselves to others, this does not produce the passions linked with the war of all against all, because natural man sees the world in a solipsistic way. He assimilates the other fellow men to mindless nature and thus is not concerned with the image that they form of him.

It follows from this reformulation of Rousseau's argument that the rise of society is connected less with the loss of natural independence and more with the entrance of other human beings within the cognitive horizon of natural man. At this point the notion of pity, the other attribute of human nature, becomes blurred. How can a being for whom other men are just a piece of nature be moved by pity for them, especially if we take it that pity involves some measure of identification with the sufferer? For Rousseau, however, the nature of this identification is such that even the animals are, to some extent, able to attain it. The difference between man and animal, with respect to pity, is just a matter of degree.[15]

C. THE STATE OF NATURE AND SOCIETY

A second series of tensions in Rousseau's argument is bound up with the demarcation of the state of nature from society. These tensions are not so much linked with Rousseau's need to minimize the cognitive endowment of natural man as with Rousseau's intent to attribute what he identifies as the corruption of contemporary man to the influence of social life. The beginning of social life is traced by Rousseau to the gradual transformation of sexual relations from a "transient commerce required by nature" to another kind of bond, "rendered more durable by mutual association." In the creation of the first family ties "men begin to consider different objects, and to make comparisons; they imperceptibly acquire ideas of merit and beauty, and these soon give rise to feelings of preference."[16] As this early form of social life begins to blossom, however, the basic sentiment of man begins to shift from 'self-love' to 'amour-propre.' Gradually men come to view themselves almost entirely in terms of their social appearance. Yet a wish to be noticed and to stand high in public esteem presupposes that people have already entered each other's world of experience. A solipsistic consciousness that regards others in the guise of "pieces of nature" cannot possibly be concerned with their esteem.[17] Hence the internal tension of Rousseau's argument.

If the desire to be noticed presupposes that men are already aware of having an identity for others, and if that desire marks the beginning of corruption, then it must be the case that a time existed when men were aware of their identities for others—and thus lived an already *social* life—but were *not yet* concerned with their status. Either Rousseau must assume the existence of a fully social but not yet corrupted condition, or he must concede that in the state of nature men not only were able to compare themselves with others, but were also aware of their image in the minds of others. The first solution is the most acceptable for Rousseau. In fact, it is conceivable for him to admit that there existed a transient moment when people were aware of each other and yet were not so concerned with their social image. If we introduce a distinction between on one hand a concern for status where the terrain, the modalities and the reward of excellence are entirely defined by society, and on the other hand a desire for excellence which derives from the necessities of the struggle for existence, then the tension disappears. We can imagine that when men grew aware of others, they also became concerned with restoring the unlimited autonomy that they formerly enjoyed. Conceivably, the desire to excel, to outdo the other and to distinguish oneself might derive from a more fundamental desire to restore one's autonomy in the absence of certainty about the benign character of the other's will. Such competitiveness, although already based on a social consciousness, cannot be considered corrupt—even by Rousseau's standards—for it constitutes simply a reaction, dictated by our natural self-love, to the discovery of other minds. Excellence in this transient social stage is pursued only for its intrinsic value for survival, whereas only in the more developed and, from Rousseau's standpoint, corrupt stages of society is it pursued for its *exchange value*, i.e. for the social advantages that it procures. In the light of these considerations the image of human nature implicit in Rousseau's discussion of the state of nature and society appears characterized by a degree of distrust much higher than the explicit picture of human nature which opens the "Second Discourse."

Some of the critics who accuse Rousseau of primitivism radicalize this objection much further. Even if we allowed for the possibility of a less corrupted form of competitiveness—so runs the objection—the fact remains that for Rousseau man cannot enter *any* type of social relation without corrupting himself. According to these interpreters, Rousseau advocates the return to the state of nature or else he contradicts himself when he proposes a political program for reforming society.[18] This line of interpretation misunderstands Rousseau in at least one respect. For Rousseau, once men have entered society there is no way back to nature.[19] Thus his ideal is to reconstitute in the emancipated society not so much the lack of awareness of others as the lack of concern for approval that is typical of the state of nature. Contrary to the primitivist interpretation, this lack of concern for approval is to be attained, according to Rousseau, not by keeping others at greater distance but by reducing social distance. Intimate relations, for instance, bring the actors closer together and yet reduce their concern for the other's valuation of their appearances. This is not to say that in Rousseau's vision of an emancipated society the social bond should coincide with intimate bonds—in that case *The Social Contract* would not have been written—but that one of the measures of emancipation is the extent to which a society does not prevent or distort relations in which the awareness of others is somehow independent of the concern for one's status.[20]

D. THE TRANSITION TO SOCIETY

A host of new problems emerge when we place Rousseau's conception of human nature into the broader context of his explanation of the transition from nature to society and of the role of man's agency in this process.

Cassirer has credited Rousseau with providing an innovative solution to the problem of theodicy. Rousseau, according to Cassirer, places the responsibility for the presence of evil in the world "at a point where no one before him had looked for it." He creates "a new subject of responsibility, of 'imputability'. This subject is not individual man, but human society.... Selfish love, which contains the cause of all future depravity and fosters man's vanity and thirst for power, is exclusively to be charged to society."[21] Cassirer, however, overestimates the extent to which Rousseau's solution is indeed a viable solution. Instead of *solving* the problem of theodicy, Rousseau shifts it

from the terrain of theology to that of philosophical anthropology. For society is to be seen as a consequence, however remote
and unintended, of human action. Thus even if we imagine its
emergence as due to fortuitous circumstances rather than to a
human propensity to "truck, barter and exchange," still we
must admit that insofar as we envision man as endowed with
any degree of self determination man must partake of the very
evil of society. This difficulty was already evident to Rousseau's
contemporaries. Charles Bonnet, a citizen of Geneva who wrote
under the pseudonym of Philopolis, objected to the "Second
Discourse" that "if the state of society derives from the faculties
of man, it is natural to man."[22] Rousseau's reply to Philopolis
suggests that he was also aware of the problem. In Rousseau's
words,

> Society is natural to the human species as decrepitude is to
> the individual. The only difference is that the stage of old age
> derives solely from the nature of man and that the state of
> society derives from the nature of the human race, not imme-
> diately but with the aid of certain external circumstances that
> could have occurred or not occurred, or at least happened
> sooner or later and consequently accelerated or slowed down
> its progress.[23]

Rousseau conceded that "many of these circumstances depend
on man's will,"[24] i.e. that man has the capacity to at least delay
their effects. This recognition, however, does not remove the
problem. For although the contribution that human nature
makes to the rise of society needs to be activated by some contingent event, nonetheless man remains responsible insofar as
he has the power to bring the process to a halt. If man proceeds
towards association, it is hard to escape the conclusion that
association meets his inclinations. However, in order to assess
whether the explanation of the rise of society contradicts the
notion of the state of nature introduced at the beginning of the
"Discourse" we have to examine Rousseau's argument more
closely.

The tranquil life of man in the state of nature was often dis-
rupted, according to Rousseau, by the occurrence of such difficulties as "the height of some tree, which prevented man from
reaching its fruits," "the competition of other animals equally

fond of the same fruits" or the fierceness of animals "that even aimed at his life."[25] These difficulties, combined with the natural capacities of man, led to the development of tools and to their intentional use on the part of man for the purpose of dominating nature. The first instrument must have been man's own body. Through careful exercise men learned how to develop their agility, swiftness and vigorousness. Then, by chance, some stones of the proper size and shape or some fallen branches must have been available at the moment when a hungry man was trying to kill an animal or to reach some fruits. Nothing more needs to be assumed, according to Rousseau, in order to account for the transition to social life. Accidentally some individuals must have come across useful objects and, under the pressure of a momentary scarcity, must have happened to go through bodily movements which resulted in the satisfaction of their need. Because man initially had no grasp of the connection between the accidental act and the relevant outcome, many such procedures were probably forgotten and discovered again countless times even by the same individual. However, it is also plausible that after a number of successes some process of learning started and the fortuitous use of tools consolidated into a stable practice. Furthermore, Rousseau assumes that the human species grew more numerous and extended itself geographically. Bad weather, long and severe winters, drought and other natural calamities must have occurred. Since they surpassed the ability of any individual to deal with their consequences, these calamities provided the first incentive for groups of men to cooperate. At the same time, argues Rousseau, the repeated application of various instruments to himself and to other things "must have naturally engendered in the mind of man the idea of certain relations," such as those expressed by the word 'great' as opposed to 'little', 'strong' as opposed to 'weak', 'swift' as opposed to 'slow', 'fearful' as opposed to 'bold', and so on. The cognitive ability to deal with these basic relations, in turn, must have produced in man "some kind of reflection, or rather a mechanical prudence, which pointed out to him the precautions most essential to his safety."[26] This prudence, in turn, increased man's ability to control the environment and induced him to feel the first emotion of pride, for instance pride in domesticating the mildest of the

animals or in killing the most ferocious. Conceivably, man started to apply his newly acquired ability for drawing comparisons
also to the other fellow human beings. Hence, "seeing that they
all behaved as himself would have done in similar circumstances," each man came to the conclusion that the others were
similar to him.[27] However, only when men grew able to distinguish the situations in which the common interest authorized
them to count on the assistance of others from the situations in
which a conflict of interests made distrust a more useful attitude did it become possible for the individual to take part in
collective endeavors which usually were prompted by new,
unexpected or larger "natural difficulties." Different types of
natural calamities, linked with the specificity of each site of
human settlement, made for the usefulness of different instruments and practices. This diversity of natural contexts eventually resulted in the diversity of the various groups of men and
the diversity of the various civilizations.

Two questions are raised by Rousseau's account of the evolution of mankind from the state of nature to the patriarchal
society. First, to what extent is such an account consistent with
the description of the state of nature offered in the first part of
the "Discourse"? Second, since this evolutionary transition represents somehow the fatal step which sets the human species
on the way to what Rousseau calls "corruption," and obviously
a step for which society cannot be blamed, to what extent is the
nature of man responsible for it?

Let us consider again the conditions under which the evolutionary step takes place. "Natural difficulties" of the kind
meant by Rousseau must have existed before the rise of society.
Therefore something else must have triggered the transition,
for example (a) the fortuitous discovery of tools, (b) man's self-
consciousness, (c) his ability to draw comparisons, or (d) his
ability and disposition to act upon rational expectation rather
than on immediate desire. Leaving aside the fortuitous discovery of tools, which of course cannot be attributed to man, and
the ability to make comparisons, whose difficulties we have
discussed above, we are left with the necessity to postulate a
powerful inclination toward rationality in natural man. Again,
this disposition goes beyond what Rousseau said about human
nature at the beginning of the "Discourse." For it must now be

assumed that even in the most primitive conditions and even in the absence of any social consciousness man is able to grasp the advantage inherent in certain *indirect* ways of seeking satisfaction. Also, in order for him to remember the procedures that once proved successful, man must already possess a propensity toward systematizing isolated facts, events or actions into broader, symbolically organized patterns of meaning. The image of man conveyed by Rousseau's account of the transition from the state of nature to society presupposes a considerably greater disposition to rationality than Rousseau's explicit picture of human nature. From a motivational point of view, however, Rousseau's account is more consis tent with his premises. Nothing beyond the desire for the satisfaction of physical needs leads natural man to make use of, and develop further, his potential for rationality.

If reconstructed along these lines, Rousseau's thought does contain a viable answer to the intricacies of the problem of theodicy. Namely, man *is* responsible for the initial step which severed him from the state of nature and gave rise to social life but, if we are willing to concede to natural man a somewhat more robust inclination to reason than Rousseau does in the beginning of the "Discourse," this claim introduces no inconsistency within the argument. From this perspective Rousseau's critique of Hobbes can also be rescued. The responsibility for the war of all against all can no more be attributed to human nature than human nature can be blamed for man's failure to foresee the consequences of taking up an instrumental-rational way of satisfying his needs.

E. FROM THE PATRIARCHAL TO THE AGRICULTURAL SOCIETY

Another source of tension for the consistency of Rousseau's image of human nature has to do with his account of the second evolutionary step taken by the human species, i.e. the transition from the early patriarchal stage to the agricultural society. From the occasional cooperation that had become possible when men left the isolation of the state of nature a rudimentary language began to develop, as well as some notion of obligation. The technical ability to build shelters brought man and wife and offspring to live together. Conjugal and parental love differentiated, and families were formed. Also "a species of property" arose, which consisted mostly of clothes, weapons and few other personal objects. People's few needs and desires were easily taken care of. Yet soon men began to use the increased amount of leisure time that their new skills afforded for acquiring a number of conveniences unknown to their ancestors and whose privation became "far more intolerable than the possession of them had been agreeable." The sentiment of love came into being, but it brought also feelings of envy and jealousy. For Rousseau this patriarchal stage of society, equally far from the "indolence of the primitive state" and the "petulant activity of egoism" typical of more developed societies, "must have been the happiest and most durable epoch."[28] But, then, why did mankind leave it ?

According to Rousseau, a major evolutionary breakthrough soon came to upset the stability of the patriarchal society. The new revolution was brought about by the discovery of metallurgy and by the advent of agriculture. The enormous impact of metallurgy and agriculture on social life is due to their requiring stable cooperation, and thus interdependence, to an extent unequaled by the simple activities through which men ordered their lives up to then. Metallurgy and agriculture also increased the productivity of human labor and for the first time made available a surplus product whose property and enjoyment became open to dispute.[29] Furthermore, the tilling of the soil must have played a decisive role in the rise of a new type of claim. By invoking the labor of his hands the husbandman could now lay a claim to the land itself. The initial year-to-year claim to the acquisition of the harvest was only a step from the full-fledged concept of property.[30] However, even if property had already become the main reward for labor, the results of this rudimentary division of labor would have remained positive, according to Rousseau, "if men's talents had been equal." But men's talents were unequal. Thus the strongest did more work, the most ingenious found ways of obtaining the same product with less ef fort and both felt entitled to more property. Through the mechanism of inheritance these inequalities of property, which initially were merely the result of natural inequality, consolidated into a socially sanctioned inequality of individual conditions. At this point a full-scale competition for social rewards developed which eventually led to the Hobbesian state of a generalized war.

Two aspects of this transition enter into tension with Rousseau's explicit picture of human nature. One of them is linked with the rise of metallurgy and agriculture, the other with Rousseau's account of the growth of the division of labor. It is very unlikely that men who could hardly take into account future needs and had no knowledge of the final product and of its potential applications should take the pains of digging out the ore, of working and smelting it. Rousseau acknowledges the difficulty. Even assuming that the sight of a volcanic eruption might have given man the idea of the smelting process, still primitive man must be attributed an unlikely large amount of "courage and foresight" in order to endure such toil while having so a vague an idea of the possible outcome. Agriculture requires even more sophisticated knowledge and motivations. In order to grow a harvest one must "consent to lose something now to gain a great deal later."[31] How to reconcile such a degree of rationality with Rousseau's image of natural man?

Similar complications affect Rousseau's account of the division of labor. In one respect, Rousseau's conception of the division of labor anticipates Durkheim's idea that the division of labor can arise only within a preexisting society.[32] For Rousseau, as for Durkheim, cooperation does not generate society, but rather presupposes it—it presupposes a society at least as developed as the patriarchy of the Golden Age. Only after some degree of association is achieved on the basis of blood affinity, geographical concentration and attachment to the land does cooperation become possible. Rousseau sees the rise of the division of labor as linked, through the requirements of large scale cooperation, with the advent of metallurgy and agriculture. As soon as some men began to smelt and forge iron, argues Rousseau, others were needed who would maintain them in exchange for iron products.[33] This explanation raises more questions than it answers. For how could those who decided to specialize in the production of iron be sure that eventually they would be able to exchange their product, if they themselves were uncertain as to the final shape and usefulness of iron? Why would they ever renounce the security of their old independence for the sake of an activity which initial-

ly would put them at the mercy of others? Nor is it clear how
they could expect to obtain something in return for their iron
before their prospective customers had any idea and experience
of its use.

The general pattern of these difficulties is similar to the one
encountered in connection with Rousseau's arguments against
Hobbes and about the rise of social life, but with one important
difference. The first transition, from the state of nature to the
patriarchal society was prompted by a combination of chance,
man's self-consciousness, man's intelligence and his desire for
food and security. The second evolutionary breakthrough is
instead characterized by a different distribution of natural factors and human agency. The role of the expedient "fortuitous
events" which enabled Rousseau to separate conceptually the
rise of society from man's nature is not the same in the two
cases. Whereas the fortuitous events which triggered the first
revolution provided man with serendipitous solutions to *immediate* and *already manifest* problems, the fortuitous events which
caused the transition to the agricultural society set in motion a
train of activities which are only *likely* to satisfy *secondary* needs
yet to arise. Consequently, the role of man's free agency in the
second revolution is far more important. Even if the needs of a
larger scale of production pressed him into a greater specializa-
tion of tasks, patriarchal man still had the power to delay or
hasten the development of the division of labor. If man has-
tened the process instead of slowing it down, it was not
because of any fatal accident, but because his desire for riches
and power had already increased to an extent incompatible
with Rousseau's picture of the Golden Age.[34]

Against the charge of inconsistency Rousseau could retort
that the patriarchal form of association constituted enough of a
social experience to push the imagination of man beyond the
limits of immediate desire. In fact, more complex needs presumably arose as soon as technical progress allowed man to
divert his attention from the satisfaction of the most urgent
necessities. These new needs, in turn, were likely to require
more time and ability for their satisfaction—hence the rationale
for accepting the risky dependency entailed by the new division of labor in lieu of the old, safe, but stifling independence.
Rousseau could admit that, after the initial break with nature,

man bears a greater responsibility for his social destiny and that no natural accidents can explain the second step of social evolution, but at the same time could contend that, starting from the moment when man broke off from nature, human nature is no longer merely natural. Rather, it is already a social product, however infinitesimal the influence of society. To be sure, at every successive turning point of social evolution man's responsibility for his destiny is greater, but the nature of the choosing person is also more thoroughly socialized. From this perspective, Rousseau could consistently explain why social evolution proceeds faster and faster in a more advanced society, and why man is willing to lose more and more of his independence as he grows more dependent on others.

F. SOCIETY AND THE SELF:
ROUSSEAU'S CRITIQUE OF MODERNITY

According to Rousseau, with the advent of the agricultural societies irreversible changes in the relations of men with one another were already under way. The combination of different natural talents with dependency and with the institution of property began to produce its effects. On the one hand, any social order structured around dependency, property and inequality is bound to generate insincerity among men. Ever since competition for rank, property or power made its appearance, contends Rousseau, "it became to the interest of men to appear what they really were not."[35] The necessity to "appear what one is really not" is rendered all the more pressing by the very nature of the rewards for which men compete, i.e. wealth, power and prestige. These rewards are identified by Rousseau as a sort of zero-sum objects. In order for the acquisition of wealth to constitute a meaningful goal, there must exist others who are not rich. Similarly, people can take an interest in power only insofar as they see the possibility of gaining power over others. Furthermore, the outcome of any competition depends among other things on what the others *believe* of us. Thus, argues Rousseau, by rewarding conformity with the existent roles and participation in the division of labor with zero-sum goods, all the past societies indirectly put a premium on cunning, on the ability to mislead and induce fear, on envy and distrust.

On the other hand, through competition society induces another distortion in human nature which is subtler and more insidious than insincerity, i.e. *inauthenticity*. Precisely because it is in the interest of men to appear other than they are, the evolution of a competitive civil society inevitably widens the gap between feeling and action, inner nature and social conduct. The fear of losing ground in the social race makes people choose the solid ground of collective representations over a toilsome search for their true motives and identity. Man becomes so dependent on the opinion of others, argues Rousseau, that his very sense of self-cohesion is endangered and the self is gradually reduced to pure exteriority, a mere copy of what society requires. At the apex of social evolution, in the Parisian society of his times, Rousseau saw a gallery of masks under which no person existed any longer. Paradoxically, under the exhilarating effervescence of a new differentiation of roles and life-styles, celebrated by Diderot as a source of new possibilities for self-expression, Rousseau perceived instead the risk of an increasing fragmentation of the individual and of an increasing conformism.[36] The Parisian life of the mid-eighteenth century appeared to Rousseau as a society where the erosion of autonomous subjectivity had gone so far that it had become almost superfluous to know the character of people in order to predict their conduct. Knowledge of their interests usually sufficed.[37] In this life-form, "as the clocks are ordinarily wound up to go only twenty-four hours," so the individuals "have to go into society every night to learn what they're going to think the next day."[38]

Rousseau's insight into the relation between the mechanism of social reproduction and the dominant character traits is one of the most valuable elements in his legacy. What remains most 'alive' in Rousseau's "Second Discourse" is not his attempt to show that society emerges "naturally from nature" without man's nature having any inclination for it. His argument to this effect could probably be revised, tightened and improved up to the point that it could meet many of the objections moved against it, but nonetheless it remains one of the most dated aspects of the Discourse. Instead, Rousseau's critique of a social reproduction based on competition retains a relevance for us. His indictment of the effects of competition goes well beyond

the themes, familiar to his contemporaries, of political unfreedom or economic injustice and anticipates the concern which,
for all their diversity, Marx, Weber and Durkheim share in common. In fact, the notions of alienation, of the 'iron cage' and of
anomie all point, from different perspectives, to the same basic
quality of modern life in the West to which Rousseau called the
attention of his contemporaries.[39] Underneath each of these
expressions is the same intent to capture conceptually the turning of the logic of instrumentalism against those elements of
the social world which at the beginning of modernization contributed to the rise and expansion of pragmatic and instrumental modes of action.

These authors tell a similar story. In early modern times
from within a traditionalistic society emerged a sphere of economic (and, for Weber, also political) action, where the principle of the maximization of utility prevailed. The autonomy of
the market and the state from the religious meanings which
integrated medieval society was made possible by the peculiarly rational quality of Western culture (Weber) and by centuries
of primitive accumulation (Marx). Up to a certain point the differentiation of these two spheres generated progressive effects,
which Weber understands as the diffusion of a rational conduct
of life, Marx understands as the unfettering of productive
forces formerly stifled by the medieval institutional order and
Durkheim sees as the increase of individuation inherent in an
organic, as opposed to a mechanic, form of social solidarity.
With the further expansion of the influence of the market and
the state, up to their eventual occupying that central place in
society that in the Middle Ages belonged to the Church, instrumental modes of action acquired an ever increasing acceptance
throughout society. At this point, so continues the story, the
effects which the terms 'alienation', 'iron cage' and 'anomie' try
to capture become visible. The hegemony of the type of social
action rooted in the modern profit-oriented enterprise and in
the bureaucratized state apparatus slowly undermines the
credibility and integrative capacity of cultural traditions, which
are then reduced to folklore and subjective convictions (Weber),
undermines the ethical attitude toward work (Weber), prevents
the majority of people from expressing themselves through the
products of their work, thereby reducing work to mere toil

(early Marx), obfuscates the intersubjective nature of social events and institutions (late Marx) or, in yet another vocabulary, undermines social cohesion through the "abnormal forms" of the division of labor (Durkheim). Underneath these various phenomena a unique pattern is discernible. That is, modern society, after a certain point in its development, begins to erode the cultural, social and psychological bases on which it rests.

Rousseau's anticipation of this theme contains two elements which set him apart from the other eighteenth-century and earlier theorists. On the one hand, Rousseau did not just distinguish between civil society and the state, as most political theorists of his time did, but *within civil society* he distinguished between *systemic patterns of action*, i.e. the unintentional influence of the existent arrangements in matters of property, stratification and division of labor, and the imperatives of *social reproduction*, i.e. of the reproduction of viable social relations, livable identities and traditions. On the other hand, whereas Smith, Mandeville and most of his contemporaries proceeded from the assumption—condensed in the metaphor of the invisible hand and in the formula "private vices, publick benefits"— of a preestablished harmony between systemic patterns of action and a well-balanced reproduction of society, Rousseau challenged this certainty and suggested that what is functional for the reproduction of the social stratification and of the division of labor may not be functional for the reproduction of social solidarity and of cohesive personal identities.

We have now followed the entire trajectory of Rousseau's argument in the *"Discourse on the Origin of Inequality."* We started with his anthropological portrait of human nature. Then we have looked at how this portrait was deformed—sometimes voluntarily, sometimes unknowingly—in order to refute Hobbes, to explain the formation of the first form of social life and to account for the first steps of social evolution. We have located the end-point of this trajectory outside the "Discourse," in the picture of modern urban life that Rousseau draws in *The New Heloise*. While this picture shows the long-term effects of the social processes investigated in the "Discourse," the other works of Rousseau can be seen as different aspects of the remedy that he recommends against these effects.

3

THE LEGITIMATE POLITICAL ORDER

The solution envisaged by Rousseau for the problem of neutralizing the effects of the modern form of social reproduction comprises two distinct aspects. On the one hand, the competitive way of distributing rewards should be overcome, or at least the process of legislation should be protected from the distorting influence of social inequality. This aspect of Rousseau's solution is developed in *The Social Contract*. On the other hand, the individual must be strengthened and made more impervious to the pressure coming from a civil society marked by inequality and the competition for zero-sum goods. In a sense, some of the self-sufficiency of natural man should be given back to the modern individual. In *Emile* and in *The New Heloise* we can see spelled out the different, yet complementary, forms assumed by what Rousseau understands as the restoration, rather than the creation, of autonomous individuality.

The important insight contained in Rousseau's concept of an emancipated social life is his intuition that neither aspect of this "dual reform" will suffice alone. That is, alienation from the self can no more be used for creating a just order than political freedom alone can deliver the individual from anxiety or inner repression. On the other hand, the pursuit of institutional transformations without attention to the character and the motivations of people is bound to generate new unfreedom, just as hopes for a merely individual liberation are destined to remain unfulfilled. What renders Rousseau's political theory relevant to the concerns of our time is his insistence on the fact that an adequate notion of emancipation must include the idea of personal *authenticity*, alongside the more traditional concepts of freedom, equality or justice, and his effort to reflect on the psychological transformations which should complement the emancipation of social relations.

However, before discussing the ethical and psychological presuppositions which underly Rousseau's approach to the subjective dimension of emancipation, I will reconstruct the main lines of his vision of the just political order. More specifically, I will be concerned with the radical egalitarianism of a Rousseauian society, the issue of Rousseau's totalitarianism, his concept of freedom and, finally, the distinction of public and private virtue. This last theme provides the link between Rousseau's political writings and the other works here examined.

A. COMPETITION AND THE EMANCIPATED SOCIETY

Rousseau's ideal arrangement for a just social order has often been interpreted as a *meritocracy*. Various passages of *The Social Contract* and of the "Discourse on the Origin of Inequality" provide evidence in support of this thesis. According to the meritocratic interpretation, for Rousseau the inequality of social position, whether it is symbolized by wealth, higher authority or marks of status, is illegitimate only if it is not "in proportion to physical inequality."[1] Rousseau's egalitarianism —so runs the argument—is not meant to level off all individual differences in matters of social standing, but merely to bring the allocation of social rewards in line with real merit. On the basis of Rousseau's statements that the absolute equality of the state of nature would contrast with the principle of distributive justice if applied to the civil society, and that all the members of society "should be distinguished in proportion to their merits,"[2] Della Volpe contends that the main contribution of Rousseau to social theory is the formulation, for the first time, of the problem of a just connection between individual merit and social rewards. In his opinion Rousseau has something to contribute to the solution of this problem, i.e. the "concept of an egalitarian yet nonlevelling society," by which Della Volpe means a society characterized by "a universal proportion of social differences and individual differences in merit (force, talent, etc.)."[3] Finally, Della Volpe compares Rousseau's notion of a just social order with Marx' notions of the socialist and the communist society. Whereas socialism, by giving equal rewards to equal quantities of labor, still levels off the individuals insofar as it neglects the different degree of effort that they must expend to produce the same amount of value, the communist society, by demanding from its members in proportion to their capacity and providing for them according to their needs, appears to place a higher value on individual differences. Rousseau's position on equality, for Della Volpe, comes closer to Marx' notion of the communist society.

Colletti exposes the confusion between merits and needs in Della Volpe's argument, but in the end falls into a similar misunderstanding of Rousseau along meritocratic lines. "Whereas Rousseau insists on the necessity for society to recognize individuals' 'merits'," points out Colletti, "Marx refers, on the contrary, to the social recognition of individuals' 'needs'." Both are somehow concerned with the proper recognition of individual diversity in the just society, but with one important difference. Whereas Rousseau "deems it necessary to take individual differences into account in order for society to be able to as sess the distinct 'merits' and consequently to structure its 'ranks' according to the 'services' offered by the individuals and thus according to their distinct capacities and performance," Marx instead "wishes that society be able in a future to take differences among individuals into account precisely in order to provide for the 'needs' of the less able and to prevent hierarchy from arising."[4]

The interpretations of Della Volpe and Colletti fail to do justice to the fundamental orientation of Rousseau's social theory. Rousseau's statement to the effect that social station should be in accord with real merit must be seen as part of a critique of the traditional, premodern order of ascriptive privilege. In this sense, the fair acknowledgement of the different contribution offered by the individuals to the reproduction of society represents an important ingredient of the transition toward a just society, but does not exhaust the gist of Rousseau's position on the matter. On the one hand, there are several passages, not only in *The Social Contract* but also in the "Project of a Constitution for Corsica" and in the "Considerations on the Government of Poland," in which Rousseau stresses the importance of socioeconomic equality among citizens in relation to the legitimacy of legislative decisions. On the other hand, it remains unclear how the fairness of competition could offset the effects of competition on social solidarity and personal identity which are analyzed in the *"Discourse on the Origin of Inequality."* Even if rendered fair through a real equality of opportunity, would competition not continue to make it in the interest of men "to appear other than what they are"?

The originality of Rousseau's position is more striking when contrasted with that of other critics of modern civil society. The meritocratic ideal which Della Volpe attributes to Rousseau fits Durkheim's position better. In *The Division of Labor in Society* Durkheim advocates what he calls *organic solidarity,* i.e. a social order where the division of labor allocates the available tasks according to the abilities so fairly that eventually the individuals end up in the social station that they deserve. From this standpoint it is possible to criticize a concrete society on the ground that it does not allocate the privileged roles in a fair manner, but it becomes impossible to criticize the existence of privilege.[5] This blindspot is typical of all meritocratic versions of the concept of emancipation. Closer to Rousseau's position is Marx' criticism of the economic dynamics of bourgeois society. Marx does not criticize bourgeois society for distributing unequally the chances of access to its leading roles, but for the radical incompatibility of the *existence* of those positions, regardless of who occupies them, with fairness and social justice. However, Marx directed his efforts to the critique of simply *one* form of competition taking place in *one* area of social action. He analyzed the social effects, and to a lesser extent the psychological ones, of a competition for wealth carried out within the privileged strata of the capitalist society by means of extracting surplus value from wage-labor. Because he considered the dynamics of this special form of competition the key to the understanding of modern society, Marx never looked at the social effects of other forms of competitive conduct centered around other goods and other sets of rules.[6] Rousseau, instead, centers his critique of modern civil society on the effects of *all* forms of competition for zero-sum goods. The originality of his position, which goes far beyond a mere demand for the equality of opportunities, is obscured in the interpretations suggested by Colletti and Della Volpe.

B. NEITHER TOTALITARIAN NOR LIBERAL

A second, and once very influential, line of interpretation accuses Rousseau of totalitarianism. Critics such as Lester G. Crocker, John W. Chapman, Charles E. Vaughan and Jacob L.Talmon[7] call attention to what they see as the overwhelming power of the community over the individual, the boundless authority of the sovereign and the *a priori* rightness of the general will. The critics of Rousseau's totalitarianism often quote the passage of *The Social Contract* in which Rousseau states that the legitimate institutional order amounts to "the total alienation to the whole community of each associate with all his rights."[8] The impression of totalitarianism is corroborated by Rousseau's suggestion that the legislator, understood as the charismatic founder of a political society, ought to feel capable of "changing human nature" and of "altering man's constitution in order to strengthen it."[9] Furthermore, the impression is reinforced by Rousseau's contention that the social contract demands a readiness to alienate to society whatever part of one's powers that society judges important to make use of.[10]

Crocker argues that since the acts of the sovereign are not bound, in Rousseau's theory, by any Bill of Rights, constitution, custom or precedent, Rousseau is in fact demanding "a total alienation of all rights to the State."[11] Crocker first of all forgets here that Rousseau understands the "sovereign" as the totality of those who have a right to participate in the formation of the general will. "The sovereign" is just another name for "the citizenry." Second, Crocker forgets that although Rousseau reconceptualizes the "natural" rights of the individual as rights *acquired* upon entering the social compact, and although the community appears then as the sole distributor and guarantor of rights, Rousseau sets definite limits to what the general will can legitimately decide.[12] These limits constitute a stronger set of checks than any liberal theorist, from Locke to Jefferson, has ever suggested to place upon the power of the polity.

The limits set by Rousseau to the general will take the form of a number of *conditions* which must be fulfilled in order for a legislative act to count as an expression of the general will of a society. Some of these conditions have to do with the *formal properties* of the object of deliberation, others concern the *social condition* of the participants and others are linked with the *motivations* of the participants in the deliberative process. The *formal* requirements specify first that what is up for deliberation must concern the common interest. This means that the object of deliberation must be of a general nature, must be applicable to all the members of society and must not contain reference to any individual or group of individuals.[13] Furthermore, even if the object of deliberation is general, the general will cannot legitimately introduce any disparity among the participants with respect to obedience to, or benefits from, the law. For Rousseau, "the sovereign never has a right to burden one subject more than another, because then the matter be comes particular and his power is no longer competent."[14] Finally, even when the object of decision is indeed general and none of the consequences of the decision results in a disparity among individuals, the general will cannot impose on the members of society burdens which are useless to the community.[15]

As regards the *social* requirements of the legitimacy of a collective decision, it goes without saying that everyone should be free to express his or her opinion. Less obvious is the fact that there should be a certain equality of wealth and power. "As to power, it should fall short of all violence, and never be exercised except by virtue of station and of the laws; while, as to wealth, no citizen should be rich enough to be able to buy another, and none poor enough to be forced to sell himself."[16] In fact, differences of opinion, according to Rousseau, are rooted in differences of interest and in turn differences of interest are rooted in differences of social condition. Rousseau lacks an articulate concept of class beyond the self-evident notion of a privileged order of citizens, but the reality of the classes works its way into Rousseau's social theory in the form of a recurrent and distinct motif.[17] That is, class divisions destroy the sense of a communal identity which constitutes the basis for the public virtue of citizens. Without a sense of community, rooted in 'pity' and in the feeling of shared historical experiences, no general interest can exist, let alone be discovered and acted upon.

Finally, the *motivational* requirement specifies that when a decision has to be made, the participants in the deliberative process are not called on to express themselves on whether the object of deliberation suits their private interests, but rather are asked to say whether in their opinion the proposed law "is conformable or not to the general will," i.e. whether in their considered judgment such a law embodies a truly general interest. This quality of the act of deliberation, together with the assumed sincerity of the participants, distinguishes a decision which reflects the general will from a *compromise* between equally particularistic ends. This distinction is captured by Rousseau with his opposition of "the general will" and "the will of all," where the latter is just the sum total of a number of particular wills.[18] The mental attitude required here of the conscientious citizen resembles quite closely the motivation later required of the Kantian moral subject in the context of choosing a right course of action. Both Rousseau's citizen and Kant's moral actor have to orient themselves to the general interest of the community, must project the consequences of a rule of action or of a political decision upon the life and future welfare of the community and, finally, must pass judgment on the desirability of those effects. Unless the citizens participate in the political process with this mental disposition and are committed to sincerity the result of the deliberation will not express a truly general will.

The combination of these requirements constitutes one of the most powerful set of restrictions ever imposed on the legiti-

macy of an act of legislation and one of the most powerful guar-
antees for the rights of the individual ever conceived. If one
compares Rousseau's concept of the social contract with that of
his predecessors, a remarkable difference emerges with respect
to the foundations of political obligation. Apart from Locke and
Montesquieu, for most of Rousseau's predecessors the factual
consent of an individual was a sufficient ground of legitimate
obligation. It mattered little whether this consent was obtained
through the pressure of external circumstances or out of a really
free deliberation. In this way, slavery and despotism could both
be justified. For Rousseau, instead, the consent of the parties
does not suffice to render legitimate a contract or an act of legislation which infringes the requirements specified above.[19]

In sum, the totalitarian aspects of Rousseau's thought are
not to be found in his theory of the general will. This theory
rather amounts to a legitimation of revolution and to an affirmation of the right to withdraw obedience from any deliberation which fails to satisfy the requirements of the general will.[20]
Moreover, recent commentators have drawn a misleading parallel between the general will and Durkheim's notion of the
conscience collective. The two concepts, according to Lukes, are
"both collective in source, impersonal in form and authoritative
with respect to the individual."[21] A double confusion is
involved here. First, whereas the general will is a *result* of association, the existence of a *conscience collective* is rather a *presupposition* of social life.[22] Second, whereas the concept of the general will is meant to provide a *normative* standard for the
legitimacy of acts of legislation, Durkheim's collective conscience is a *descriptive* concept rather than a standard. In fact,
when Durkheim takes the collective conscience as the ultimate
frame of reference for making sense of the meanings shared by
a community, he thereby renders the further questioning of
those cognitive and moral orientations meaningless. For how
could we be sure of the validity of the standpoint from which
we criticize the collective conscience if not, in a circular way, by
reference to the contents of that collective conscience which we
are trying to criticize? In a sense, Durkheim's concept comes
closer to the notion of the *life-world* as understood in the phe-
nomenological tradition than to Rousseau's intent to construct
a critical standard.[23]

In other areas, however, Rousseau's political theory is indeed ambiguous and does expose itself to the accusation of totalitarianism. These ambiguous areas include the formation of one's considered judgment on the generalizability of interests and the substantive determination of the common good. For Rousseau, all public discussion is inherently dangerous. Ideally, the people should be "adequately informed" about the issue under deliberation, but the final resolution should be agreed on "without any communication among the citizens." The formation of the general will is linked with public opinion, but with a public opinion "which coincides with unreflected opinion, i.e. with opinion in its prepublic state." Thus Rousseau ends up with a notion of "democracy without discussion."[24] Furthermore, suggests Rousseau, public opinion can be mistaken and often needs to be "guided." While the general will is always just and fair,

> the judgment which guides it is not always enlightened. It must be made to see objects as they are, sometimes as they ought to appear; it must be shown the good path that it is seeking, and guarded from the seduction of private interests.[25]

The need for guidance becomes more disquieting when Rousseau links it with the roles of the legislator and the censor. Sometimes, argues Rousseau, the principles and arrangements which would further the harmonious development of society are beyond the comprehension of those who must make the decision. The prudent quality of these principles and solutions may not be self-evident or it may not suffice to make them accepted. Whenever this is the case the legislator should resort to "an authority of a different order, which can compel without violence and persuade without convincing."[26] Beside appropriating and making use of the authority of religious symbols, the legislator is advised to privately concern himself with "manners, customs and above all opinion," i.e. the areas of shared meaning which contribute to the strength and vitality of the state. A similar train of thought underlies Rousseau's suggestions on the issue of censorship. Rousseau has been accused of advocating a kind of thought control,[27] but this represents a distortion of his ideas on the subject. Any decision of the censor remains ineffective, argues Rousseau, if it does not reflect the people's opinion.[28] Rather than molding people's opinions, for Rousseau the censor plays the role of interpreting and lending institutional legitimacy to the existing mores.

The last chapter of *The Social Contract*, devoted to civil religion, is also pervaded by a totalitarian overtone. Rousseau recognizes, indeed anticipating Durkheim, that only with the support and legitimation offered by the symbols of the sacred can a political society achieve durable stability and cohesion. After reviewing the social implications of various types of religious faiths, he proposes a "civil" religion as the most suitable form of religion for the purpose of stabilizing the order of the social contract. The articles of faith of the "civil" religion are simple. They include the belief in the existence of a Deity, in the immortality of the soul, in the happiness of the just and the punishment of the wicked, as well as the condemnation of intolerance.[29] The acceptance of these articles of faith must be demanded of each citizen, whereas those who merely pay lip service to its dogmas should be punished by death. Crocker rightly points out that what matters to Rousseau, in the end, is not the truth of religion but its coercive and emotional powers. A manipulative tone is indeed associated with Rousseau's discussion of civil religion. Even more dubious and implausible, in Rousseau's theory of civil religion, is the notion of a self-manufactured belief, i.e. the idea that people could decide which religious beliefs to establish and then proceed to believe them in earnest.

C. ON ROUSSEAU'S CONCEPT OF FREEDOM

In spite of the passages where an authoritarian use of power is suggested, *The Social Contract* constitutes an advance over the liberal tradition of Natural Law and over the Lockean theory of the *Two Treatises of Government*. The advance is represented by Rousseau's formulation of a new concept of freedom. In a famous essay, Isaiah Berlin has captured the opposition between liberalism and other types of social theory, including Rousseau's notion of the social contract, in terms of the contrast between a "negative" and a "positive" conception of freedom.[30] The former refers to the degree to which one is not impinged upon by other human wills. "Negative" freedom is the experience of having no external power influence one's will, or the substanceless virtuality of open options. "Positive" freedom, instead, is the freedom to realize the best of one's potentialities, to become a human being in the fullest sense of the word. This second concept of freedom implies a striving toward emancipation which remains absent from the first. The notion of positive freedom not only includes a denunciation of the fetters which constrain our action, but also points to some direction for our strivings. This notion of freedom, which underlies Hegel's philosophy of history as well as his view of the development of *Geist* and is implicit in Marx's historical materialism, stresses the question of who or what determines our actions, whereas the notion of negative freedom focuses on the strength and the area of application of heterodetermination.

By positing a new relation between liberty and equality, Rousseau reshapes the constellation of liberal values. The liberal opposition of freedom and equality has always generated difficulties. Too much inequality in social life is morally repulsive, not to mention the risks that it involves for the preservation of freedom. Yet if effective legislation is to be devised in order to promote economic and social equality among all the citizens, then the freedom of the most fortunate and prosperous citizens must be somehow curtailed. The dilemma is well stated by Berlin:

> If the liberty of myself or my class or my nation depends on the misery of a number of other human beings, the system which promotes this is unjust and immoral. But if I curtail or lose my freedom, in order to lessen the shame of such inequality, and do not thereby materially increase the liberty of others, an absolute loss of liberty occurs. This may be compensated for by a gain in justice or in happiness or in peace, but the loss remains, and it is a confusion of values to say that although my 'liberal', individual freedom may go by the board, some other kind of freedom —'social' or 'economic'— is increased.[31]

This difficulty arises, however, only if our conception of economic activity and of civil society already prejudges the answer to the question: Should everyone be free to accumulate wealth?

Rousseau works his way out of the liberal paradox by arguing, against the protestation that in order to promote equality "the freedom of some must at times be curtailed," that in fact those few, whose freedom should be diminished in the name of equality, have limited in the past and are limiting now the freedom of all others through their pursuit of wealth. In fact, because of the zero-sum nature of wealth, anyone who onesidedly accumulates riches produces a situation in which all the others are forced to either follow suit or face an "impoverishment without loss." Critics who discount this argument as yet another instance of the archaic economic views of Rousseau and reproach him for seeing the economy as a closed and static system, fail to understand that the converse assumption of an expanding economy by no means invalidates Rousseau's point.[32] For the success of an individual in gaining control of a larger share of the expanding wealth makes the others' share *proportionally* smaller than it would have been otherwise. When the relative gap between the wealthy and the poor grows wider, it is indeed a small consolation—*pace* Rawls—to realize that today's share is anyway larger than yesterday's. The same reasoning applies to the pursuit of power. The fact that physical aggression is seen by all liberal theorists as an instance of impinging upon the freedom of others, whereas the pursuit of wealth and power is not, only shows the bias inherent in liberal theory. As the prohibition of physical assault cannot be construed as the curtailment of anybody's freedom, neither can the policies directed at curbing the unlimited accumulation of wealth. Instead of speaking of negative and positive freedom perhaps one should speak of an *internal polarity* between, on the one hand, a concept of negative freedom which allows for the unilateral pursuit of zero-sum goods and, on the other hand, an equally negative notion of freedom which forbids such activity because it impinges, albeit indirectly, on the liberty of all the others.

There is a sense, however, in which Rousseau's notion of freedom comes close to Berlin's "positive" freedom. For Rousseau freedom never means merely the freedom to do what one wants. It could be the case that in the just society the general will will regulate, discipline or perhaps restrict the area of free action to a larger extent than any present society. Yet

Rousseau would consider this an *expansion* of freedom. Now, this type of freedom resembles positive freedom because it is achieved through the creation, as opposed to the keeping under check, of political institutions, yet by freedom Rousseau means precisely "being one's own master" in the sense of not having one's life depend on external forces.[33] According to Berlin, however, insofar as it contains an element of "positive" liberty, Rousseau's conception of freedom would be bound to presuppose a view of the human being as split between a higher and a lower self. The higher self in this view is identified with the "ideal," the "rational" or the "autonomous" self, whereas the lower self is equated with "irrational impulse," "uncontrolled desires," the "actual" or "heteronomous" self, which needs "to be rigidly disciplined if it is ever to rise to the full height of its 'real' nature."[34] It is unfortunate that Berlin's argument on freedom should generate such implausible conclusions when applied to the case of Rousseau. In fact, if there is at all a tradition of thought which views the human being as the locus of a struggle between reason and impulse, between understanding and desire, between a calculating self and the blind force of the passions, that is precisely liberal thought from Hobbes to Locke, from Berkeley to Hume and to Smith.[35] On the contrary, one of the most significant aspects of Rousseau's work is his rejection of this view of the self, his contention that the splitting of the self into conflicting segments stems from social conditions rather than from nature, and his insistence on the necessity to reconcile the rational and the affective moments of the modern individual.

Let me point to another sense in which Berlin's dichotomy fails to do justice to Rousseau's political theory. According to Berlin, the split between the "noble" and the "base" self, typical of the "positive" conception, entails the equation of the noble self with something larger than the individual, be it a community, a tribe, a race, a class or a state. Such an entity is then seen as the only "true" self which, "by imposing its collective, or 'organic', single will upon its recalcitrant 'members', achieves its own, and, therefore, their, 'higher' freedom."[36] According to the positive view it is right sometimes to coerce people for their own sake, i.e. in the name of interests or ideals which they would themselves pursue if they were more enlightened, or less ignorant, or less corrupt. In spite of his use of infelicitous expressions such as "forced to be free," Rousseau can hardly be criticized from this point of view. It is true that the general will sometimes "must be made to see objects as they are," or even "as they ought to appear," and that for Rousseau sometimes the people must "be taught to know what they require." However, since it cannot be assumed that having an interest in social change always coincides with being aware of that interest, all theories inspired by an emancipatory intent include reference to some 'pedagogic' process of enlightenment and to some agent—be it the philosopher, the radical intellectual, the party or the legislator—who initiates the learning process. The presence of such a figure per se constitutes no threat to liberty. What is decisive is whether the superior vision of the pedagogic agent includes also the right to *act* on behalf of the yet-to-be-enlightened. Because for Rousseau a political decision is valid only if it is general in scope and made in a condition of near equality by citizens oriented to the common good, under no circumstance can a particular will be *legitimately* imposed on anyone on the ground of its expressing the will of a "true self" or anything of the kind. Even though sometimes the legislator can take up an anticipatory role and indicate the common good to those who are not yet in a position to see it, nonetheless the ultimate validation of a decision rests on nothing else than the positive recognition of the citizens. The absence of such recognition may be due the imperfect realization of the requirements of the social contract or to other historical contingencies, but in no case has anybody the right to take action on what is still *only by supposition* a general interest.

Rousseau's *procedural* conception of the legitimacy of political decisions, according to which political decisions are valid and binding not by virtue of their conforming to a substantive idea of the good, but by virtue of their fulfilling a set of formal conditions, presupposes a concept of freedom which partakes of both moments of Berlin's dichotomy.[37] This concept of freedom embeds a concern for guaranteeing the individual against the illegitimate decisions of authority, but also includes a concern for transcending the view of freedom as mere absence of constraint. By implicitly relying on this new concept of freedom, Rousseau broke away from the Natural Law tradition. At the same time, by separating the legitimacy of a political order from its justification in metaphysical or substantive terms and by linking this legitimacy to the formal, social and psychological qualities of the context within which the order is created, Rousseau anchors his political theory to that *principle of subjective freedom* which Hegel, in his *Philosophy of Right*, identifies as the basis of modernity.[38]

D. CIVIC VIRTUE AND PRIVATE VIRTUE

Among the classics of political theory, *The Social Contract* is the one in which more attention is paid to the relation between the individual and the community. Within his concept of the emancipation of social relations, Rousseau brings together the fulfilment of the person and the advancement of freedom in the community. Yet in *The Social Contract* Rousseau links, as the classical political theorists did, the good polity with the promotion of virtue among the citizens. Rousseau's relation to classical political theory, however, is a complex one. He adopts Aristotle's idea that the goodness of a political order must be measured against its capacity to enhance the morality of the citizens[39] and, accordingly, rejects Machiavelli's and Hobbes' reformulation of the central issue of political theory as concerning the most effective way to secure the political survival of the state. However, Rousseau parts ways from the substantive conception of the good presupposed by Aristotle and looks for a more abstract and formal foundation of political right.[40] Also, the relation between civic virtue, the just society and the private morality of citizens is complex. Rousseau takes a very 'realist' view of the common good. The general interest is not an abstract notion or a regulative idea in the Kantian sense, but is rather the tangible result of the existence of the good community. The general interest must really exist before we can identify it and translate it into legitimate norms and, in order for it to exist, it must continuously be recreated by the social practice of the community. If a rigid system of class induces stable tensions between groups of citizens, then there may not be a common interest after all. Furthermore, the existence of the good community is a necessary condition for the institution of the social contract to function because only such community provides a social and psychological environment where the disinterested attitude indispensable for discerning the general interest can develop. Then another difficulty of Rousseau's political thought becomes manifest. A just society, in which only general interests are institutionalized as norms, promotes the moral virtue of its citizens, but the social contract cannot operate unless the citizens are already virtuous.

This circularity is a recurrent aspect of all theories of society based on an emancipatory vision. Ironically, it underlies Hegel's *Philosophy of Right* just as much as Marx's *Critique of Hegel's Philosophy of Right*. More generally, can the relation between good institutions and required motivations be transformed into a virtuous circle of normative progress, in which the efforts of individuals who are moral innovators bring about better institutions and these, in turn, stimulate higher levels of moral motivation, thus creating the conditions for yet another normative advance? World-historical individuals who are capable of bringing about institutional changes by channeling powerful collective motivations (for Hegel), or the ability of the proletariat to acquire class consciousness and transform social relations in the direction of the classless society (for Marx), are examples of factors deemed capable, despite the opposite direction to which the theories of these two authors point, to perform the same function—namely, to bridge the gap between the contingent inadequacy of the available motivations and the motivations required by the just society. It is through the actions of these subjects of history that the inertia of the existing arrangements can be broken through.

Rousseau's social and political theory is haunted by the same question. His answer is not to be found in *The Social Contract* which, being a philosophical inquiry into the foundations of political right and obligation, contains neither political recommendations on the subject of the transition to the just institutional order nor an elucidation of the intermediate stages of this transition. Again, as the argumentative thread followed by Rousseau in the "*Discourse on the Origin of Inequality*" led us beyond the boundaries of the "Discourse," so the question implicitly raised by *The Social Contract* can receive an answer only if we are prepared to look for this answer in other parts of Rousseau's work, especially in *Emile* and *The New Heloise*. This task will be carried out in the next two chapters.

Finally, let me add one more consideration on Rousseau's totalitarianism. Contrary to what some of his critics have maintained, for Rousseau civic virtue cannot be equated with the supreme good of an overpoliticized society. Rather, from *The Social Contract* emerges a vision of the emancipation of social relations which cannot be reduced to the dimension of civic virtue alone. Alongside civic virtue, a noncivic and nonpublic sort of virtue is indispensable for the purpose of making legitimate decisions in all the situations where the pressure of competition and social class is still effective.[41] Such *private* virtue, by which we are roughly to understand the acquisition of an autonomous morality of principle complemented by authenticity, is not an unfortunate second best. Rather, insofar as (1) the just institutions cannot by themselves induce the attitudes necessary for their functioning, (2) almost everywhere social conditions remain marked by striking inequalities of fortune and power, (3) particularistic interests continue to influence public decisions and (4) people are often not aware of their real motives, the attainment of private virtue becomes a crucial requisite for the development of a responsible civic virtue. No greater misunderstanding could skew one's reading of Rousseau than to attribute him a desire for the politicization of all aspects of social life. If anything, the overall emphasis of his work —even of his work as a political theorist—points to the limitations of the political as a privileged terrain for the emancipation of social life.

4

ROUSSEAU'S PSYCHOLOGY OF THE SELF

Let us now turn to the second aspect of Rousseau's "dual reform," i.e. the acquisition of *private* virtue. How can the self be made more impervious to the effects of a competitive society without isolating it from all social relations? How can moral autonomy and personal authenticity be attained? The answer to these questions is sought by Rousseau in the direction of education and "personal reform" toward an authentic conduct of life. In this chapter I will reconstruct the main lines of the educational program which, according to Rousseau, can lead an individual to acquire an autonomous moral conscience. This program is based on a metaphoric parallel between the history of the species and the development of the individual, makes a systematic use of the notion of psychological stage and rests on an implicit psychology of the self which I will try to bring out in the second section of the chapter. Some of Rousseau's most valuable insights are to be found in this implicit psychology and in the use to which Rousseau puts it in his ethical views.

A. EDUCATION VERSUS SOCIALIZATION

In *Emile* Rousseau investigates the contribution that an appropriate education can offer to the consolidation of the identity of the modern individual. He calls his pedagogic suggestions a program for "negative education." From a strictly pedagogical point of view, negative education means that no direct attempt to shape the child's beliefs, character and morality is allowed and that the task of the educator consists in creating a social and emotional environment where the child's potentialities can unfold without constraints and outside the influence of society.[1] The idea of negative education is expressed by Rousseau through the image of a sapling in the midst of a highway. Without the protection afforded by an appropriate education the child is, like the sapling, exposed to prejudice, authority, "bent hither and thither and soon crushed by the passers by."[2] In this image are condensed all the similarities and differences between Rousseau's and Locke's theories of knowledge and of the development of the human mind. Both Locke and Rousseau believed that initially, at the beginning of the species as well as at the moment of birth, the human mind is a blank slate on which our contacts with the external world inscribe perceptions and ideas of increasing complexity.[3] Yet whereas Locke (and later Condillac and Helvetius) understood the image of the blank slate as conveying a critical, antidogmatic and emancipatory conception of man, Rousseau held the opposite opinion. For Rousseau, plasticity and impressibility are the most dangerous properties of the human mind. For if the mind is shaped by the environment and our thoughts are reflections of the external world, if the human mind comes inevitably to fit the order of the world-as-it-is, then also the arbitrariness of unjust social arrangements will perpetuate itself through habit. However, this preoccupation—which anticipates the central concern of the later German idealist philosophers in their opposition to the empiricist conception of knowledge—does not lead Rousseau to reject the Lockean theory of knowledge.[4]

From a sociological point of view, "negative" education means that the goals of education should be kept separate from the goals, values and prejudices which prevail in the larger society. *Emile* is not going to be socialized into any role or set of social expectations, but will be educated to become an autonomous person. No matter which social station he will come to occupy, "he will always be in his right place."[5] Rousseau contrasts the objectives of traditional and negative education as the conflicting notions of "élever un homme pour lui-même" and "l'élever pour les autres." Rousseau's negative education is really a *critical* education in that it prepares the child for membership in an ideal society not yet existing and radically different from the society that the child will actually encounter as an adult. This idea, accepted and subsequently emphasized by Kant,[6] has been overlooked by Durkheim who attributed to Rousseau the "positive" and quite unlikely goal to "put the child in harmony with his social environment."[7] Negative education can finally be seen as an education for moral autonomy. If the learning process results in the passive internalization of social norms on the part of the child, this entails the failure of negative education. Instead, a good education implies, for Rousseau, that the child develops the ability, and the disposition, to submit all the received norms and expectations to the scrutiny of his or her moral principles. Moral autonomy in the end will become so much part of *Emile*'s character, that the others will perceive it as an *authentic* morality as well.

If we question further the idea of negative education from the perspective of its implicit developmental psychology, we encounter Rousseau's notion of an orderly sequence of stages whose characteristics and pace must be respected by the educator. The preceptor must adapt the form and content of his teachings to the specific abilities, motivations and modes of social control which characterize the various stages. Above all, the educator must never try to have the child anticipate performances which are appropriate only at a later stage. Of course, the idea of the psychological development of the child as the acquisition of increasingly complex competences and the idea

that education has to adjust to the graduality of this process
were not entirely new. Locke, depicted by Rousseau somewhat
unfairly as the advocate of "positive education" and of "reasoning with the child as with a grown-up," had already insisted on
the opportunity to fit the educational method to the age-specif-
ic maturity of the child.[8] Nevertheless, Rousseau must be credited for being the first to understand the psychological development of the child in terms of a series of *discrete* stages and for
anticipating concepts and theories which will appear in a
developed form only in our century.[9]

The development of the child is described by Rousseau in
terms of five stages. In the *first* stage only nonverbal interaction
with a nurturing figure is possible. This is the stage of *infancy*,
extending from birth to the onset of speech. At this stage, no
individuation or selfconsciousness exists and the movements
and reactions of the child are pure reflex. Even though the baby
has no cognitive grasp of itself, the vicissitudes occurring during this period of life influence, according to Rousseau, the
quality of the subsequent affective life. For instance, Rousseau
argues that breast-feeding is desirable not just because of the
physical properties of maternal milk, but also because of the
"tenderness" and love which a mother can thereby communi-
cate. This primal empathy of the mother is so indispensable for
the future development of the ability to love that, in Rousseau's
words, if the "voice of instinct" is not strengthened in the child
through habit and empathy, then "the heart dies, so to speak,
even before being born." The baby's experience of maternal
empathy is the first experience of love and constitutes for
Rousseau the emotional basis out of which all the other feelings
will later develop. At this stage, the general maxim to be followed is "to allow the child to contract no habits." Teaching
consists in the manipulation of the physical experience of the
baby for the purpose of preventing certain ideas from taking
hold of the child's mind. For example, one should give or
refuse an object to the child depending on whether the child is
silently reaching out to it or is loudly crying for it. At all rates,
it is better to carry the child to the object than to bring the
object to him. In this way the child will learn "not to give commands to men, for he is not their master, nor to things, for they
cannot hear him."[10]

The *second* stage of growth goes, according to Rousseau, from the acquisition of speech to the beginning of adolescence. This is the time of childhood proper. Whereas the first stage was characterized by the extreme weakness of the infant in relation to the environment and by its total dependence on others, with childhood the child's needs begin to be balanced by his or her abilities.[11] The faculty of understanding begins to develop, although it remains tied to the sensory imagery of concrete perceptions, i.e. to what Rousseau calls "la raison sensitive."[12] Memory remains limited, because our ability to recollect past events voluntarily is linked, for Rousseau, with our capacity for judgment and, at a stage when the child can perceive objects but not form complex ideas, judgment is still undeveloped.[13] This is not to say that children are governed only by sensory stimuli. On the contrary, according to Rousseau they can reason quite well about things which affect their "*actual* and *sensible* well-being."[14]

Two pedagogical consequences follow from these psychological considerations. First, the *content* of education, in order to be appropriate to this stage, must be restricted (a) to the training of sight, hearing, touch, smell and taste, (b) to the training of the motor apparatus through physical exercise and (c) to the development of physical coordination in general. Given the child's inability to form complex ideas and the limitations that this inability imposes on memory, Rousseau discards as pointless the teaching of any subject which presupposes elaborate notions, such as history, ancient or foreign languages and moral precepts. Instead, subjects which rest on abstract logical relations among ideas, such as geometry, can be presented to the child, if the educator recasts their logical and deductive form into a sort of inductive exercise. Geometry, for example, can be taught by leading the child to discover the properties of the basic figures from concrete experiences.

The second consequence has to do with the appropriate method for delivering the teachings. Apart from a number of practical hints, such as avoiding the use of books and always referring to concrete experiences, Rousseau's main prescription concerns the basic concept underlying the learning process. The idea of *natural necessity* is the only conceptual ground which the educator can use for providing justifications for his teachings.

At this stage, according to Rousseau, children are not ready to grasp any notion of utility or morality. They can only understand the idea of *necessity* in the sense of a stable causal connection between phenomena which eventually result in pain or pleasure. This idea constitutes an advance over the direct and immediate experience of pain and pleasure typical of the first stage. Now children can anticipate, and to some extent master, longer sequences of events from an instrumental perspective. Their goals, however, are and should remain limited to one overarching aim, i.e., survival or the satisfaction of basic physical needs. For Rousseau, the preceptor must be especially careful to keep separate, in his reasoning with the child, the notion of natural necessity from the idea of necessity as rooted in the human order of things—namely, as it stems from power, authority or obligation. To adapt to the first kind of necessity does not mean to renounce one's freedom and the child's character cannot receive any harm from doing so. However, to give in to the will of another human being inevitably engenders in the child loss of self-esteem, lust for power and a proneness to corruption. Hence Rousseau advises the educator to "keep the child dependent on things only" and to let the unreasonable wishes of the child meet with physical obstacles only or with "the punishment which results from his own actions."[15] Again, this Rousseauian idea is later echoed by Kant, who in his treatise on education, contends that "the *will* of children must not be broken, but merely bent in such a way that it may yield to natural obstacles."[16]

Finally, the educator at this stage must not only refrain from having recourse to any notion of obligation or obedience, but also must try to prevent the child from coming in contact with any idea of morality. Then, of course, one of the difficulties of Rousseau's educational program concerns the proper method of controlling the child. The preceptor, prohibited by Rousseau to explicitly direct the child, has to act from behind the scene and manipulate his pupil into performing the right action as though the child were merely responding to natural events. To those who fear that such prohibition to issue commands might undermine the preceptor's ability to control the child, Rousseau answers that no subjection is so complete "as that which preserves the form of freedom" and that the pupil must be left in the illusion of being the master while, on the contrary, both the environment and his or her conduct are under the control of the preceptor.[17] This solution to the problem of discipline has incensed many critics of Rousseau. Many have taken issue with the manipulatory flavor of the relationship between the educator and the child and some have objected that if Rousseau's program can count as an "education *for* freedom, certainly it is not an education *through* freedom."[18] Apart from the issue of manipulation, the whole idea that the child could grow psychologically without depending to any extent on the empathic response of a significant other, or that he could construct an identity merely by mirroring his self against things and natural processes, seems rather dubious. Moreover, the child comes to be affected by the educator's indirect response anyway, and if the educator responds to his pupil in terms of aloofness, hostility or withdrawal of love, but never in a positive and approving way—as it can be gathered from a number of anecdotes presented by Rousseau as exemplary solutions to the problem of control—then the educator's conduct will produce even more insecurity and emotional dependency in the child.

The *third* stage of growth, which takes place approximately between age 12 and age 15, is characterized by a favorable reversal of the balance between needs and abilities. The child's abilities develop so rapidly that he or she now has, according to Rousseau, a surplus of energy and intelligence to be spent for tasks other than the satisfaction of immediate needs. Sexuality, in Rousseau's picture, has not yet entered the scene and thus the surplus of inner resources can be entirely used for a number of developmental tasks.[19] At the same time another advance takes place in the area of understanding. The "raison sensitive" now gives way to a full-fledged faculty of understanding, capable of inductive reasoning. This inductive reasoning can now be detached from the limited context of immediate needs and can sustain endeavors of broader scope. At the same time, the conceptual basis of the child's understanding is enlarged from grasping merely the necessity of natural causal processes to conceiving the utility of certain courses of action. Means-end relations between complex sequences of actions can now be mastered by the child. This provides the educator with a new ground for justifying his teachings to the child. Such new ground, constituted by the notion of utility, becomes viable from a motivational point of view because now *curiosity* arises in the child.[20] Rousseau suggests that at this stage a great effort should again be made not to expose children to concepts, ideas or theories that they have not themselves discovered from experience, and not to have them learn more words than they can master ideas.[21] This precept is all the more valid now that the child has access to complex ideas. Through reference to concrete experiences and examples the child can be taught geography, mechanics, anthropology, chemistry, natural history and astronomy. At the end of this stage, if the correct method has been followed throughout, the educator should be able to reap the first fruits of his work. Now

> Emile knows little, but what he knows is really his own; he has no half-knowledge. Among the few things he knows and knows thoroughly this is the most valuable, that there are many things he does not know now but may know someday.... He is large-minded, not through knowledge, but through the power of acquiring it; he is open-minded, intelligent, ready for anything, and, as Montaigne says, capable of learning if not learned.... Emile's knowledge is confined to nature and things. The very name of history is unknown to him, along with metaphysics and morals. He knows the essential relations between man and things, but nothing of the moral relations between man and man.... He only judges what is outside himself in relation to himself, and his judgment is exact and certain. Caprice and prejudice have no part in it. He values most the things which are of use to himself, and as he never departs from this standard of values, he owes nothing to prejudice.[22]

The *fourth* stage of development extends from age 15 to age 20. It is the age of reason and also the age of the passions. According to Rousseau, the awakening of sexuality and the setting in of moral conscience are the two crucial aspects of this stage. Consequently, the task of the educator is twofold. On the one hand, the educator must facilitate the interaction of the emerging sexuality with the natural sentiment of pity, on the other he must stimulate the moral growth of the child.[23] The two drives are complementary. When accompanied by the energy of the sexual impulse, pity can turn into an impetuous sentiment of affection, and the sexual impulse can be ennobled by pity. From the conjunction of the two emerges the capacity for friendship and then for love. From pity derives also a sentiment of sociability and the desire to associate with other persons. These feelings, together with the rise of *conscience*, render the child mature enough to fully enter the social world. ·

A few words on the concept of conscience are perhaps necessary. Various statements to the effect that the "decrees of conscience are not judgments but feelings" might suggest that Rousseau tries to go back to a naturalistic morality or grounds ethical precepts in a psychology of the moral sentiments.[24] Such an impression is dispelled if one places Rousseau's discussion of conscience in the broader context of his polemic against the rationalist view of morality that was typical of the natural law tradition. Rousseau's concept of conscience is meant to fill the gap opened on the side of motivation by the excessive rationalism of Pufendorf's approach to morality. Against such a view Rousseau contends that reason can indicate the good to us, but cannot provide us with the motivation to act on the recognition of the good. That requires instead a sentiment as strong as the passions which lead man toward evil, and to this sentiment Rousseau gives the name of conscience.[25] Rousseau's morality, however, is not a morality of the good sentiments, but a morality of reason. For him conscience without reason is incapable of generating right conduct, because only through our reason can we identify what is right to do. In a letter to M. de Francquières Rousseau offers a very clear, and almost Kantian, distinction between goodness as defined by the approval of conscience and virtue as defined by reason. Writes Rousseau:

> To do good is the most enjoyable pursuit of a generous man. His honesty, his benevolence are hardly the effect of his principles; rather they are the result of his goodheartedness. He gives in to his inclinations, when he acts justly, just as the villain gives in to his own, when he acts wick edly. To appease our propensity to good amounts to goodness, but not to virtue.[26]

Returning to Rousseau's educational program, we note that the preceptor is faced at this stage with the problem of leading the pupil into the world of moral action without relying on abstract ethical concepts that the youth cannot yet understand. The study of history, suggests Rousseau, will prove helpful. For it can offer the child the opportunity to examine the motives of other people without the risk of getting entangled in real-life situations which might hurt him. Furthermore, the combination of participation and distance afforded by the study of history will enable Emile to get acquainted with base motives without becoming himself base or cynical.[27] Again, positive models are to be avoided. No matter how commendable and exemplary the lives of the great men can be, Emile should never be put in the position to desire to be somebody other than himself. Finally, also this stage is characterized by an optimal outcome. Whereas at the end of the third stage the child should be able to form an autonomous judgment on the utility of objects, activities and processes, at the end of the fourth the child should possess (a) a capacity for autonomous moral judgment and (b) a capacity to choose love objects independently of their external, social image.

The *fifth* and last stage—called by Rousseau "the age of wisdom and marriage"—roughly corresponds to early adulthood. It extends between age 20 and 25. No crucial psychological developments take place during this stage, but only a gradual maturation of the abilities that Emile already possesses. At this time Emile meets Sophie, the woman educated according to Rousseau's precepts; he falls in love and decides to marry her. The education that Rousseau envisages for Sophie stands in a strident contrast with the guiding principle of his educational philosophy. Whereas Emile is educated for himself, Sophie is educated for another, i.e. for pleasing her future husband. Rousseau maintains that women are "specially made for man's delight" and that their inferior reason condemns them to be "at the mercy of man's judgment."[28] Women should not be deprived of education, in Rousseau's eyes, but their education should emphasize "only such things as are suitable," for example grace and delicacy of feeling, wit, artistic ability and craftmanship with no pretense of creativity, common sense, modesty and religious piety. The preceptor, however, demands that Emile postpone marriage until his education as a citizen is completed. This final segment of Rousseau's curriculum, from which Sophie is exempted, includes travel and exposure to other cultures, to the life of the city, to politics and to the reality of social inequality. The book ends with Emile married and about to become a father. Emile thanks the preceptor and asks to be now assisted in educating his own children in the same way.

Although some of Rousseau's ideas about child-development can still be taken seriously today, many of his concrete suggestions are little more than curiosities—for instance, his idea that sexuality arises with puberty, or the idea that the child could dispense with all notion of morality up to adolescence. However, buried under the pedagogic and dated surface, there is a core of interesting themes and intuitions in Emile, constituted by an implicit psychology of the self.

B. ROUSSEAU'S PSYCHOLOGY OF THE SELF

The central tenet of *Emile* is that the development of the self occurs in stages and that optimal development consists of meeting a series of challenges of increasing complexity in a successful and autonomous way. The complexity of the life-challenges with which the child is faced, however, does not increase in a continuous way, but takes the form of sudden leaps from one level to the next. As we have seen, Rousseau distinguishes five stages in the development of the individual, but underneath these "explicit" stages it is possible to identify three more basic stages, which are less arbitrarily defined and coincide with the three distinct levels of complexity of the lifechallenges that the child has to face. At the first of these basic stages, the life-challenges are comprised within the polarity of *pain* and *pleasure*. Later, once we master a few life-preserving strategies, we grow able to deal with the new problem of the *usefulness* of means to ends. Finally, after having acquired mastery of instrumental modes of action, we gain access to a third range of challenges linked with the opposition of *right* and *wrong*.[29]

The postulation of these basic stages allows us to ˙˙nderstand better the logic underlying Rousseau's conception of psychological development and the sequence of his pedagogical prescriptions. Although they differ in important ways, Rousseau's first and second "explicit" stages are really two aspects of the same developmental segment, i.e., two moments of our grasping the causal necessity inherent in some processes which result in pain or pleasure. Within this segment of their growth children learn how to master means-ends relations, but the end is invariably the child's own well-being and the means usually stand in simple relations with one another and with the overarching goal. Accordingly, at this basic stage education consists of teaching *adaptive* responses rather than trying to stimulate the child's attempts to change the environment.

The second basic stage—coextensive with Rousseau's "explicit" third stage—requires not only educational methods geared to an increased capacity for formal and abstract reasoning, but also a realignment of the learning process along the line of formal rationality. Whereas in the preceding stage only the choice of *means* was relevant, now the child is required to evaluate also the rationality of *ends* in the light of a system of preferences. The ends are seen as part of a hierarchy of choices, where each step is made necessary by and assessed against higher goals, but no reference is yet made to the moral merit of the various ends and preferences.

Finally, in the third basic stage—corresponding to Rousseau's fourth and fifth "explicit" stages—the child is required to evaluate his conduct from a *moral* point of view. The challenges to which the child must find an autonomous solution revolve now around the problematic relation of one's goals to the goals and intentions of similar beings operating in the same environment.

Even when reconstructed along these lines, the psychology implicit in Emile contains a number of dubious assumptions. For instance, Rousseau's views about the timing of the transition from one stage to the next are bound up with many prejudices of his times, especially in matters of sexuality. Also quite foreign to us is the idea of a sequential ordering of the *rise* of each new type of competence. Perhaps Rousseau should not be taken too literally in this respect. Often he seems to imply that children have no capacity for moral reasoning before their instrumental abilities are fully developed or that they cannot grasp instrumental relations before their adaptive responses have undergone a full maturation. Yet it is hard to deny that the child's responses oriented to self-preservation already contain some kind of instrumental relation and, furthermore, that the child's interaction with the preceptor obviously includes a moral, albeit rudimentary, dimension. However, in order to justify his sequential ordering of various educational methods, Rousseau needs to make only the weaker claim that the child cannot attain *autonomy of judgment* at one level (e.g. at the level of instrumental rationality or of practical reason) before he has learned to autonomously respond to the challenges of the preceding level.

Beside controversial or disputable points, the developmental psychology implicit in Emile contains two interesting and influential ideas which still have some relevance for us. The first is the idea that the path of individual development mirrors the path followed by the human species in its gradual detachment from nature. For Rousseau there is something universal and the same time something unique in the relation of each individual to the sequence of the three basic stages. There is something universal to the extent that every human being goes through these stages in the same order as the species did, but there is something unique in that we repeat that sequence under circumstances and in response to challenges that are different for each individual. Through the notion of stages Rousseau can articulate in new terms the relation between the social and the natural aspects of the human being. What social man shares with natural man is ultimately the orderliness of his psychic development.

The second idea concerns the effects of finding an original or innovative solution, as opposed to following a model solution, to the life-challenges that we are faced with. As the species had to devise original solutions for the problems which arose out of its collective experience, and was led by this cultural inventiveness to evolve far beyond all the other species, similarly the outcome of individual growth is going to be different, for Rousseau, depending on whether the individual has been allowed to respond autonomously to the various challenges or had to conform to ready-made solutions. In the first case a sense of self-cohesion and inner strength is the result, in the second rigidity, conformism and eventually a sense of fragmentation arise. There is little awareness, in Rousseau, that roles and social expectations not only constrain the identity of individuals within certain boundaries, but also *sustain* it, that they require comformity but at the same time constitute the background against which one can pit oneself and define one's identity. There is little understanding, in Rousseau, of the fact that the human self "arises through its ability to take the attitude of the group to which he belongs,"[30] and this lacuna is perhaps part of reason why today his work is rarely used within social theory.

This last remark brings us to the notion of the self presupposed by Rousseau. Rousseau lacks an explicit and coherent concept of self. In "The Creed of a Savoyard Priest" the terms 'identité du moi' and 'moi' refer indistinguishably to the perception of a demarcation of one's being from the environment and of a temporal *continuity* of one's being.[31] A different notion is conveyed by other passages, where the self (le moi) is presented as an entity capable of being appreciated or despised, esteemed or criticized for its inner structure.[32] More meanings can be found if one looks at the way in which the term "moi" is primarily used in the *Discourse on the Origin of Inequality* and in *The Social Contract*. We can find passages where Rousseau refers to that part of the individual which sees itself through the eyes of the community, participates in institutions, performs roles and worries over its social image. Yet it is possible to locate passages where Rousseau considers the self more as a source of *responses* to the expectations of society than as the locus of their passive internalization. From a Meadian perspective, sometimes the Rousseauian self comes too close to the me and sometimes it appears as an *I* which denies all relation to its *me*. More meanings can be detected if we look at Rousseau's use of the term 'self' from the point of view of psychoanalytic theory. Sometimes he uses the term to refer to the individual's idea of what his or her self *ought to* be like, i.e. to something close to Freud's *ego ideal*. For example, when Rousseau criticizes the competitive mode of social reproduction the gist of his critique is that under the pressure of competition the individuals end up flattening their ideals of self to the models embedded in social roles. At other times, instead, Rousseau uses the term 'self' to designate the *actual* self. In this sense, the self has the capacity for matching or failing its ideal, and thus for deserving esteem or contempt. Also, it is perceived as either *fragmented* or *integrated*. In *Emile* the term 'self' often has this meaning.

What determines whether an individual perceives his or her self as cohesive or fragmented? The perception of a coherent self is, for Rousseau, the product of another aspect of the person. Obviously, he lacks a conceptual equivalent of the Freudian *ego* or any notion of some internal agency capable of integrating our present self-perception with the images of our abandoned past selves and of our anticipated future self.[33] The *function* of such agency, however, is clearly present and is what Rousseau tries to capture with his concept of autonomy. Autonomy in solving life-problems—a capacity that the environment *forced* upon pre-social man and that it has now become the task of negative education to *cultivate* in the child—plays in Rousseau's conceptual framework the same role as "ego strength" in Freud's. Namely, it designates a property of the individual psyche which is largely the key factor in the consolidation of the self and in the growth of a sense of its cohesion and vigor. Rousseau is keenly aware of the consequences of the *lack* of autonomy on self-perception and he offers a vivid description of these effects in his portrait of Parisian life. Whoever as a child has been forced to conform to external expectations, as a grown-up will become whatever society, the current fashion or the reference group want him or her to be. His or her sense of self will disperse across a range of actions equally extraneous, and will be accompanied by feelings of unreality, of lability and of centerlessness—it will resemble the perception of the self, described by Peer Gynt, as an onion whose layers can be peeled off one by one only to discover that the core is itself void.

In the light of these considerations Rousseau's views on education can be reassessed. Apart from his unfortunate suggestions on the strategies to be used for controlling the child, Rousseau's project of negative education bears important similarities to Freud's vision of the therapeutic process. In both practices we find a dyad interacting on a very intense and exclusive basis. The members of the dyad do not enjoy a full equality of rights nor do they stand in the same relationship to the crucial resource—namely, knowledge. This asymmetry could be easily manipulated to the detriment of the less powerful member of the dyad. Thus both practices include the prohibition for the higher ranking member of the dyad to impose his own views, evaluations or judgments on the other person. Least of all can the analyst or the preceptor propose models for imitation. Failure to comply with this fundamental norm results in the failure of the therapeutic or educational process. Furthermore, the leader of the dyad must take an active role in somehow sheltering the patient or the child from the influence of normative demands coming from the external environment. Even the analyst, who in principle must take no part in the patient's life outside of therapy, does play an active role in protecting the patient's self-determination insofar as he or she brings to the patient's attention the social constraints or the biographical influences which impinge on the choices at hand. Both the analyst and the preceptor help the other person to deal with the social world without being representatives of society.[34] Rather, they are the representatives of a part of the person's self which has not yet come into being. Finally, both practices aim at enhancing self-cohesion and identity and both pursue this end through the strengthening of the person's *autonomy*. For both Freud and Rousseau, autonomy, in the sense of the extent to which our choices are really our own and we can take responsibility for them, is what makes a person *normal* or *mature*.

Beside the cognitive and moral development reconstructed above, for Rousseau the individual undergoes also a sort of *character* development. This development is not seen in terms of stages and is considerably less in focus, but its outline is nonetheless visible. With maturation, a distribution of strong and weak areas of the personality sets in. These are areas of conduct in which the person is better able or less able to exercise autonomy. For Rousseau, people differ both in the distribution of such areas and in the overall extension of these areas of autonomy. Such differences result in individual differences of character and generate also distinct types of self-perception. Individuals with a larger share of areas of autonomy perceive their self as stronger and more integrated than those whose areas of autonomy are more limited. The distribution of areas of autonomy, and consequently also the gap between the ideal and the actual self, is rooted in the circumstances which make of each person a unique individual. Among the individuating factors, Rousseau points to the unique features of the context in which the life-challenges decisive for each person have appeared, to the unique quality of the feelings connected with the solution of such problems and to the unique quality of the objects to which these feelings attached. As autonomy metaphorically marked the function of the *ego*, in Rousseau's implicit psychology the role of the *id* is played by the individuating circumstances which characterize the life-challenges faced by the child. Such circumstances create feelings and urges which, in turn, are at the basis of our deviations from our ideal self. These feelings and urges for Rousseau are part of our *real* self and contribute to our individuation just as much as our conscious or autonomous projects do.

Thus for Rousseau the discrepancy between the ideal and the real self is not simply an undesirable imperfection to be eliminated through a more determinate exercise of the will. On the contrary, this discrepancy is related to a complex of motivations, largely unconscious, which we must understand and accept, and by no means try to suppress or instrumentally control. Any attempt at mastering these motivations without fully grasping the coherent pattern underlying them is bound to result in a mere displacement of their effects and in the undermining of the individual's identity, as Rousseau suggests through the case of Julie. No morality and no solid identity are possible, for Rousseau, without understanding the nature and the force of the centrifugal motivations which tend to lead us away from our ideal self. This is why autonomy, although it constitutes a necessary ingredient of private virtue, does not exhaust the meaning of it. Rather, it emerges from a reconstruction of Rousseau's psychology that the private virtue called for by the just society must include also a number of other qualities, which I group under the name of *authenticity*. Among these additional qualities is a capacity to distinguish the aspects of a person's inner world which are crucial to the identity of the person from those which are expendable, knowledge of oneself, empathy, a capacity to accept emotionally the undesired aspects of one's real self, and the courage to follow one's moral intuitions even when it is difficult to translate them into the language of abstract reflection.

However, the acquisition of this complex of qualities, complementary to the acquisition of autonomy, falls outside the scope of *Emile*. Authenticity cannot form the object of "teaching" because it requires a continuous reflection on one's way of

interacting with others and thus the cultivation of real-life relations. And Emile can develop these qualities in the context of
his relation to Sophie but not so much within his relation to the
preceptor as Rousseau describes it. Furthermore, in *Emile*
Rousseau focuses on the independence of the mind from the
prejudices of society and from the will of other persons, whereas the acquisition of authenticity requires a reflection on the
relation between an *already autonomous* will and one's identity.
This aspect of Rousseau's view of the self and of morality can
be reconstructed from *The New Heloise*, but, before discussing
Rousseau's novel, let me briefly outline the sense in which I use
the term authenticity.

C. EXCURSUS ON AUTHENTICITY

An impressive philosophical lineage and its existentialist con-
notations make of authenticity a concept not easy to handle,
and in the context of this work it is impossible to review its history. I will be concerned, instead, with a much more modest
task. That is, I will try to demarcate the sense in which the term
authenticity will be used here from three concepts which are
closely related to it but should remain distinct. These three
related notions, often used in the literature on contemporary
modernity or on contemporary ethics, are *sincerity, autonomy*
and *intimacy*.

I take sincerity to mean, in a broad sense, the avoidance of
being false to anybody by virtue of being true to one's self. One
of the best characterizations of the opposition between sincerity
and authenticity is offered by Lionel Trilling. "Society," writes
Trilling, "requires of us that we present ourselves as being sincere, and the most efficacious way of satisfying this demand is
to see to it that we really are sincere, that we really are what we
want our community to know we are. In short, we play the role
of being ourselves, we sincerely act the part of the sincere person, with the result that a judgment may be passed upon our
sincerity that it is not authentic."[35] Why not authentic? Because
our being true to our self in this case is not an end, but merely a
means. As Archbishop Whately, of Dublin, once observed, honesty is usually the best policy, but those who follow this maxim
are not honest. Authenticity, we could say, is sincerity for its

own sake.[36] Furthermore, whereas authenticity is implicitly a critical concept, which calls into question the received and habitual opinion—"aesthetic opinion in the first place, social and political opinion in the next"[37]—sincerity carries no polemical implications against the social order, but often consists of what Hegel called "the heroism of dumb service."

A second way of distinguishing sincerity and authenticity hinges on two distinct modes of relating the social and the private dimension of the self, typical respectively of premodern and modern cultures. In premodern times the ultimate unfaithfulness to one's self was to try to appear other than one ought to be, i.e. to infringe the expectations linked with one's position in the social structure. This is *insincerity*. With modernity a reversal of values has occurred. The person who adheres totally to his or her social position or role, and grounds his or her identity on it, appears as the ultimate embodiment of *inauthenticity*.[38]

Finally, we can distinguish the notions of sincerity and authenticity in terms of the different attitude toward *emotion-work* that they presuppose. If *emotion-work* is understood as the act of trying to change in degree or quality an emotion or feeling,[39] then we can conceive of sincerity as the coincidence of feeling and expression which results from successful emotion-work. Authenticity, on the contrary, can be understood as the coincidence of feeling and expression in the absence of any attempt to shape our feelings. From this perspective, we can see the difficulty which inheres in contemporary ethic. If we assume that the possession of spontaneously ethical feelings depends on biographical contingencies which are at least partially beyond the actor's control, then the moral actor will often be in a predicament where the demands of *ethical rightness* as defined by principled ethics and the demands of his or her own *authenticity* diverge. The person then will have either to perform emotion-work over his or her feelings, thereby undermining the worthiness of their eventual coincidence with conduct, or follow these feelings at the cost of infringing certain ethical principles. About this tension, which constitutes the essence of the tragic in our times, more will be said in the chapter on *The New Heloise*.

Autonomy is another concept that often is not distinguished sharply enough from the notion of authenticity, especially by those who have tried to accredit Rousseau as a precursor of Kant and have stressed the convergence of the two with regard to the impersonal, formal quality of the ethical principle.[40] Understood as *ethical* rather than psychological concepts, autonomy and authenticity share an outright opposition to all traditional or premodern notions of the right, which either anchor the specification of the right in the will of some higher authority (be it God, the king, or the community itself) or define the right as the furthering of some good which can be known *a priori*. For all ethics centered around autonomy or authenticity, instead, the right has to do with the actor's capacity of following consistently a *self-imposed* principle, chosen in view of its quality of being generalizable. At this point, however, the two conceptions of ethics part ways. Every ethic of autonomy places a greater emphasis on the total coincidence of right conduct and the ethical principle. Moral worthiness here implies a total reconciliation of action and reason which at times may prove painful for the actor's feelings, but is seen as in principle always possible. This conception of ethics is best stated by Max Weber in one of the letters that he wrote as the editor of the *Archiv für Sozialwissenschaft und Sozialpolitik*. In 1907, when the first echo of Freud's psychoanalytic approach was beginning to resound, somebody submitted to Weber a manuscript for publication in which the author advocated, among other things, that husband and wife should maintain independent sexual lives and that marriage was a repressive institution. Weber, although personally interested in Freud's work, rejected the manuscript with an unusually long and emotional letter, in which he also wrote:

> we can separate all ethics, whatever their material content, into two large groups. One makes principled demands on a man, which he is generally not capable of meeting, except in great high points of his existence, and which direct his striving into the infinite: the hero-ethic. The other is modest enough to accept one's everyday 'nature' as the maximum demand: 'average ethic'. It seems to me that only the first category, the 'hero-ethic' can call itself idealism, and under this category belong both the ethic of the old unbroken Christianity and the Kantian ethic. Both these ethics start with such a pessimistic—yet appropriate to their ideal—evaluation of the 'nature' of the average individual that the Freudian discover-

ies from the realm of the unconscious have nothing 'frightening' to add. But insofar as the 'psychiatric ethic' only makes the demand: admit what you 'are', what you have desired, it really makes no new demands of an ethical nature.[41]

The theme of self-transcendence as a kind of Faustian striving regarded as good in and of itself encompasses the whole passage. There is no goal or predefined end-point at which the individual may feel entitled to rest and release the tightness of his self-controlling attitude. Rather, the ultimate end is the striving itself, the exercise of discipline and of control over the impulses. The meaning of this striving consists less in what it allows us to reach than in what it allows us to get away from, namely unmediated naturality and especially immediate inner nature.[42]

The ethic of authenticity, instead, takes a broader view of ethical rightness. Right conduct is not directly equated with adherence to formal principles, such as the categorical imperative, or with the willingness to abide by these principles come what may. Rather, right conduct stands in a more complex relation to principles. This is because every ethic of authenticity starts from the assumption that human beings inevitably have contradictory internal forces which pull them away from their self-chosen principles. Indeed, it is part of everyone's experience to occasionally give in to these inner urges and later regret it. If we feel guilty and try to bring ourselves back in line, this is certainly because—as the ethic of autonomy emphasizes—our conscious self does strive for coherence and moreover sees adherence to an ethical principle as indispensable for coherence, but—retorts the ethic of authenticity—we should not locate our true self merely at the point where action and principles fully coincide. In order to be a fully moral being, according to the ethic of authenticity, we must not deny or try to suppress, but rather acknowledge the presence and the force of the urges which deflect us from our principles, while at the same time continuing to orient our conduct to a moral point of view. As a well-known practitioner of psychoanalysis once wrote, "the salvation of man lay[s] not in becoming better through struggle with his evil side but in becoming more aware of the intense ambivalence of all intentions and behavior, i.e. in becoming less sincere and more authentic."[43]

The difference between the two ethical approaches regards the value to be attributed to our deviations from the ethical principle. For the ethic of autonomy *all* these deviations subtract something from the worthiness and dignity of the person—the less deviations the better, no matter how a life-plan which brings deviations to a minimum affects the cohesion and vitality of a given person. The ethic of authenticity, instead, introduces a distinction between deviations which are bound up with essential aspects of a person's identity and, on the other hand, deviations originating in feelings or emotions which occupy a peripheral place in a person's identity. Whereas in the latter case the actor should try to modify his inclinations or disregard them, in those cases when essential aspects of one's identity are at issue, a similar attempt is bound to result in self-destruction. In such cases the normative force of principles can be somehow suspended. Again, this opposition will be clarified by our reading of *The New Heloise*.

Finally, let me comment on the relation between authenticity and intimacy. All remarks on this relation would be superfluous, were it not for the fact that in the literature on the postmodern syndrome the notion of authenticity often tends to be confused with an ideal of disinterested intimate relationships.[44] The contemporary emphasis on personal growth as a path to authenticity is then reduced by the neoconservatives to an amoral search for mutual self-revelation. It it obvious, instead, that the two concept are to be sharply distinguished. While intimacy is a quality of relationships, authenticity is a property of conduct. One could have intimate relations without authenticity, for example on the basis of mutual sincerity. Moreover, one could conduct oneself according to authenticity in one's dealings with strangers, acquaintances and other nonintimate persons. Finally, one could orient one's conduct to the value of authenticity without even desiring to enter intimate relationships. No matter how arduous to reach in practice, a solitary authenticity is not in principle impossible. However, the two notions are also linked in one important respect: namely, intimacy is a fertile terrain for the development of authenticity. Intimate relationships are conducive to authenticity because they possess three features which set them apart from other types of relationships. First, whenever there is intimacy between people then communication somehow regards, even indirectly, identity. True intimacy requires a willingness on our part to offer our own deviations from the ideal self up for scrutiny, comment or occasional criticism, and to accept the vulnerability linked with this openness. Second, intimacy requires that we accept the other person regardless of the vicissitudes of his or her social persona and that such acceptance be bestowed in a wholesome manner. Within intimate relations, our acceptance of somebody cannot be conditional upon, or restricted to, single aspects of the self.[45] Third, intimate relationships follow the nonstrategical reciprocity of a *gift economy* applied to emotional gifts, i.e. to gifts of disclosure, of vulnerability and of access to one's identity.[46] These three features of intimate relationships are conducive to authenticity in that they all facilitate the disclosure and expression of parts of the self which normally would be kept secret for fear of disrupting one's social image.

We are now in a position, on the basis of these distinctions between authenticity, sincerity, autonomy and intimacy, to reconstruct the ethical implications of Rousseau's novel *The New Heloise* and, more specifically, his view of the relation of moral autonomy to identity.

5

BEYOND THE LIMITS OF AUTONOMY: ROUSSEAU'S ETHIC OF AUTHENTICITY

The New Heloise takes up, in a sense, where *Emile* leaves off. In *Emile* Rousseau was concerned with preserving and strengthening the autonomy of the individual through an appropriate education. In *The New Heloise* he explores the limits of autonomy as a moral value. To the extent that a novel can be 'about' anything, *The New Heloise* is about the relation of self-realization to morality. The popularity of this novel in the late eighteenth century is to be attributed, to a large degree, to the novelty of this psychological theme more than to its literary qualities.[1] Also today, the interest that *The New Heloise* can still command is linked almost exclusively with the insights into the psychology of morality that it contains.

Presently, *The New Heloise* is little read in English, for a number of reasons. First, translations are few, far from excellent and not readily available. Second, the readers of Rousseau in English-speaking countries are split into two main camps. Rousseau the political theorist and, to a lesser extent, Rousseau the theorist of education, are discussed within the social sciences, where perhaps too much attention is paid to the "liberal or totalitarian" controversy and too little is devoted to the implications of his literary works. On the other hand, Rousseau the literary author is largely studied by historians of literature and specialists of eighteenth-century French literature who pay much attention to the connection of Rousseau's themes with his personality and his biography, but take little or no interest in his social and political theory. *Emile* is a no man's land where the two groups of interpreters occasionally come in contact. *The New Heloise*, relatively neglected by the literary scholars in favor of *The Confessions*, is ignored by the social theorists.[2] Third, the interpretation of Rousseau as a precursor of Kant—an interpretation which has been very influential until recently—has further contributed to drawing attention away from *The New Heloise* and redirecting scholarly interest toward *The Social Contract* and *Emile*. Thus, before trying to outline the significance of the novel for the theme of authenticity, I will briefly summarize its plot.

A. *THE NEW HELOISE*

The New Heloise is the story of a triangle where the husband is really the illegitimate third party. The novel, written in the epistolar style made fashionable by Richardson, opens up with the mutual declaration of love of Saint-Preux and Julie, the two protagonists. Saint-Preux is the preceptor of Julie, a commoner of temperamental generosity but with no social or economic standing.[3] Julie d'Etange is the only living child of a nobleman who pins on her marriage many of his hopes for salvaging the ailing fortunes of the family. Given the foreseeable complications of their love, Saint-Preux offers to leave town, ostensibly in order to divert the danger of a scandal, but in fact in order to probe the depth of Julie's feelings. Julie, advised by her cousin Claire, whose role throughout the novel resembles that of the chorus in the Greek tragedy, asks him to stay and becomes his secret lover.[4] Saint-Preux and Julie enjoy a moment of bliss, but the seeds of divergent, and later conflicting, attitudes are already present. Julie aims at "the delicious pleasure of a platonic passion" and from the beginning writes to Saint-Preux that she needs love but her senses "have no need of a lover."[5] On the other hand, Saint-Preux's love is more passionate and more sensual. Whereas for him the obstacles to their love are all external, in the prejudices of society, Julie's feeling is always connected with guilt and shame.

It has been observed about Julie's constant speaking of shame and guilt that it masks an attempt to minimize her responsibility by attributing her misdoing to some sort of error or weakness, and that whereas Saint-Preux's passion is *intensified* by the condition of social isolation and condemnation, "Julie's fear of being uprooted from her settled position makes her cling more tenaciously to the ideal of an innocent happiness."[6] Julie, however, promises to Saint-Preux to do all that she can in order to make their common wish come through.

To make things more complicated, Lord Edouard Bomston, a rich English friend of Julie's father, comes to visit the d'Etange family from Geneva. He and Saint-Preux it is sympathy at first sight, but soon Saint-Preux suspects that Lord Bomston might be secretly negotiating to marry Julie. Tension increases, a misunderstanding occurs, tempers flare up and Saint-Preux challenges Lord Bomston to a duel. The duel is eventually avoided, but the situation has become very volatile. Saint-Preux's presence is noticed by Julie's father, who has returned home from his military life, and he begins to inquire into Saint-Preux's reasons for being in the house. Lord Bomston, meanwhile reconciled with Saint-Preux and informed about the unfortunate love between him and Julie, out of a generous but inconsiderate impulse, decides to intercede with Julie's father. The Baron d'Etange disdainfully rejects the prospect of a marriage between Saint-Preux and Julie. The scandal is about to erupt and, through Claire, Julie intimates to Saint-Preux to leave town. Promptly Saint-Preux sets off to Paris, accompanied by Lord Bomston.

We reach here the turning point which bears a direct relation to the theme of authenticity. Lord Bomston, partly out of his sympathy for the lovers, partly out of a desire to compensate them for the consequences of his *faux pas*, offers Julie a large estate in Britain where she might live with her lover if she is prepared to abandon her family. Lord Bomston is aware that his offer to Julie will be taken as an act of betrayal by the d'Etange family and indeed will be condemned by the whole town. Anticipating Julie's hesitation, he tries to convince her with two arguments. The first argument classically contrasts the pettiness of conforming to the community's mores with the dignity of inward ethical autonomy. If you remain, says Lord Bomston to Julie, sooner or later your father will arrange a marriage for you. At that point "you will be forced to contract an alliance disavowed by your heart. Public approval will incessantly be contradicted by the cry of your conscience." In the end, admonishes Bomston, you will be "respected but contemptible."[7] The second reason that he advances constitutes the first example in the history of Western ethic of a new kind of moral argument, i.e. the argument from the standpoint of the requirements of an identity. "You shall never efface love's strong impression," warns Lord Bomston, "without at the same time effacing all the exquisite sentiments which you received from nature." In the end, continues he, "when you'll have no more love left, nothing worth esteem will remain in you either."[8] The novelty of Julie's tragic predicament, on which the novelty of Bomston's argument rests, consists in the fact that she is caught not between two conflicting norms or imperatives, but between an "autonomous," self-imposed moral precept—namely, the prohibition to intentionally cause one's parents to be unhappy—and a *feeling* which is not endowed with normative force in her eyes, but on which her self-identity somehow depends.

Bomston's idea of a "duty to one's love" is rejected by Julie in the name of the old dichotomy of duty against inclination. Julie senses somehow that the decision she is about to take will have broad consequences on her identity, but she rejects the offer of Lord Bomston, protesting that the remorse for deserting her parents would be unbearable. She would prefer to be the cause of her own rather than her parent's unhappiness.

New events come to accelerate the pace of the plot. Julie's mother, secretly sympathetic to Julie's love, suddenly dies and

Julie feels guilty for having somehow contributed to her death. It is then easier for the Baron d'Etange to talk his daughter into marrying Wolmar, an elderly, noble, wise, rational and impassible friend of his to whom he owes his life and has already promised Julie's hand. The confrontation between Julie and her father goes beyond the issue of marriage. The baron speaks the language of social convention and of the code of honor. He has given his word trusting that Julie would comply with it, but her refusal now brings dishonor on himself and the entire family. In a very emotional scene the old baron kneels down in tears before Julie and implores her not to destroy his reputation and the peace of his last years. Julie begins to waver. She had resisted her father's threats, but the sight of his humiliation overwhelms her. Julie concludes that, regardless of the consequences for her own life, she really has no right to pursue her happiness at the cost of her father's despair. Such a happiness would be undeserved and tainted by guilt. She decides to terminate her relation with Saint-Preux and to marry Wolmar.

From this point on, the novel revolves around the intricate justifications and rationalizations elaborated by Julie in order to maintain a sense of self-cohesion and identity. Her first strategy is a Stoic retreat into the inviolability of her inner self: that is, she will accept Wolmar as the master of her outward life but not of her heart. Later, on the day of the wedding, Julie realizes that this is an untenable illusion. A life of insincerity is also against morality and cannot possibly lead to happiness. Then, upon entering the church, an emotion never experienced before takes hold of Julie. The sight of the altar, of the minister, of her father, of the whole place, the solemnity of the organ music, everything—as she reports in her letter to Claire—elicits awe in her and a great dread of the idea of perjury. Julie describes her state in those moments as "a sudden revolution inside," in which her chaotic emotions were being shaped aright "according to the law of duty and of nature."[9] As a result of her conversion Julie can take pride in the fact that the image of Saint-Preux no longer haunts her fantasies. Now she calls her love "extinguished" and at one point refers to it as "l'erreur d'un moment."[10]

After her conversion Julie also reconsiders all her ideas on marriage, love and the family. It is a mistake, she writes to

Saint-Preux, to think that love is indispensable to a happy marriage: instead, "honor, virtue, a certain conformity, not so much of stations and ages as of characters and temperaments, are enough between two spouses." Such a union may not be blissful, but it will certainly generate a mutual affection "no less pleasant than durable." More should not be demanded of marriage, since, continues Julie, people do not marry "in order to think exclusively of each other, but in order to fulfil the duties of civil society jointly, to govern the house prudently" and "to rear their children well."[11] On this basis her relation to Wolmar is seen by Julie as an example of moral virtue and as a standard against which she judges her past love for Saint-Preux. About Wolmar she writes in a letter:

> no illusions predispose us toward each other; we see each other such as we are. The sentiment which joins us is not the blind ecstasy of passionate hearts but the immutable and constant attachment of two respectable and reasonable people who, being destined to spend the rest of their days together, are content with their lot and try to make it pleasant for each other.[12]

In the end Julie persuades herself that if she could go back in time and choose again on the basis of the feelings of that moment, but with the knowledge of the present, she would not choose Saint-Preux but Wolmar. She closes her letter asking Saint-Preux to cease writing to her.

Upon receiving the letter Saint-Preux threatens to commit suicide and only with difficulty is persuaded by Lord Bomston to embark on a ship headed for the South Seas. After four years of adventures, adversities and experiences of all sorts he returns and, in a letter to Claire, expresses his desire to visit Julie at Clarens—the new residence of the Wolmars. Informed by Claire, Julie and her husband invite Saint-Preux to spend some time at their estate.

Much has been written about the Wolmars' way of life at Clarens. In the thematic structure of the novel Clarens, shown to us through the eyes of Saint-Preux, symbolizes the repressive autonomy which Julie has chosen to embrace. Life at Clarens is extremely orderly, almost compulsively rational. The small society of Clarens is polarized into two camps: on one side Julie and her husband, and the servants on the other. The masters, however, are of a special kind. Their domination aims at captivating the minds of the servants, not just at obtaining their services. As Saint-Preux reports, at Clarens when a new servant is hired he is offered two wages. One, the wage that is currently paid in the village, is offered to him or her in exchange for standard services. The other is a higher wage which will be paid only to the extent that the masters are really satisfied with his or her services. Very often the value of the services performed by the servant in order to obtain the higher wage exceeds the value of the extra wage. The male servants are rigidly separated from the females and a great care is exercised to the effect that their schedules never allow servants of different sexes to spend time together. When the men are off duty they are so tired that they have no desire to engage in the leisure activities attended by the women.[13] Also, leisure activities are planned by the masters with an eye to their utility. On Sundays, after the sermon the servants are allowed to assemble in the courtyard and play various games. Money is not allowed as a prize, but Julie and her husband provide some useful object for that purpose, such as some small piece of furniture or old clothes. Depending on the value of the prize, it will be awarded after one or more sets of games. These games vary so as to assure that people will develop dexterity at different kinds of tasks. Julie and Wolmar always attend these games, decide on the rules, on the prize and on who is allowed to participate.[14] Disputes and arguments among the servants are forbidden, because of their bad effect on the morale of the household. A reciprocal aversion between two equally excellent servants is usually a sufficient ground for immediately firing one of them. In this way each servant has an equal interest in making himself liked by all others and they all control one another. This mutual control is made even tighter by the obligation to denounce to the masters any infringement of the rules on the part of a fellow servant. Whoever sees another servant harming the masters' interest, and does not report it, is considered even more culpable than the wrongdoer.[15] In order to discourage calumniation, however, the denouncer is required to provide evidence of having first brought his complaint to the attention of the offender himself. If he has not, then he is reproached for having judged the motives of an action without inquiring into the actor's intentions. If the accuser refuses to bring such evidence, then he and the accused person are both put under strict surveillance and "soon one finds out which one of the two was wrong."[16] Social mobility is discouraged at the Wolmars' estate. The ideal is not so much to favor changes of social position, as "to make everyone happy in his own."[17]

This soft and captivating form of tyranny forms the background of Julie's and Saint-Preux's reunion—a reunion which comes to be dominated by the same theme of a duplicity disguised as transparency. Wolmar wants to stably integrate Saint-Preux at Clarens by offering him to become the preceptor of his children. The presence of Saint-Preux would finally complete the realization of his and Julie's aspiration to make of Clarens a "very intimate society" where all their close relations are reunited. Before making his proposal, however, Wolmar wants to make sure that all passionate feelings between his wife and Saint-Preux are extinguished. For this purpose he devises a number of tests, the last of which consists of having Saint-Preux and Julie remain alone for a week.[18] Julie is haunted by doubts about herself and writes an ambiguous letter to Claire, in which she professes self-confidence but at the same time discusses at length the best ways to avoid a resurgence of her love.[19] Claire suggests to her cousin to meet Saint-Preux as if no such danger existed, but at the same time exhorts her to take a host of precautions such as interrupting affectionate and long conversations, surrounding herself constantly with her children, and forcing herself to keep a journal of the encounters with Saint-Preux with the intention of finally showing it to her husband.[20]

The first day proves very unsettling. Julie and Saint-Preux go out on a boat trip on the lake near the estate. A storm forces the small party onto the other shore. While the boat is being repaired, the two enjoy a moment of tranquil tenderness. Julie holds Saint-Preux's hand for a while but then, overwhelmed by the fear of her own emotions, she suddenly proposes to go back and join the boat crew for the return trip. No overt mention of their feelings takes place between the two former lovers, only indirect clues suggest the intensity of Julie's and Saint-Preux's emotions. For instance, while they sit close together on the boat, sailing in the dark and cold waters of the lake, a homicidal-suicidal fantasy occurs to Saint-Preux. It is so powerful and tempting that he has to leave Julie and move to the bow of the boat for the rest of the trip. When disembarking he becomes aware of the turmoil that Julie also has experienced. After this first encounter, the rest of the week elapses in a calm and uneventful way. Wolmar comes back and life resumes its normal course, in a mood that Saint-Preux describes as convivial and characterized by silent sharing and mutual acceptance.

The situation seems to evolve toward a point of equilibrium. Claire, now a widow, agrees to move to Clarens and be part of the intimate society, and the Wolmars try to encourage a closer relation between her and Saint-Preux. However, a secret uneasiness has meanwhile continued to affect Julie. In one of her most introspective letters, she writes to Saint-Preux about her feeling of being surrounded by "reasons to be happy" without being capable of enjoying anything. Julie laments that a "secret languor" and feelings of emptiness have taken hold of her, but she closes her letter protesting that these feelings are to be attributed to her "excessive happiness."[21] The plot culminates with the accident that takes Julie's life. During a walk along the shore one of her children falls into the water. Julie dives into the cold lake and saves her child, but subsequently catches pneumonia. In a few days she develops a high fever and lets herself die opposing almost no resistance to the disease. Her death is witnessed by a whole chorus of servants and supplicants who regard her as a saint and follow the events with trepidation. In her deathbed Julie's virtuous shell and her real self come apart. At this extreme moment she begins to view her pursuit of virtue as an illusion and a rationalization which now can be cast aside. In her last hour, Julie understands and accepts the validity of the prophecy of Lord Bomston. By trying to suppress her sentiment for Saint-Preux she has set her life in accord with her idea of rightness, but this forcible act of self-mastery has failed to enhance her inner life. Virtue, after all, was not on the side of virtue, true morality was not on the side of autonomous principles.[22] It would be incorrect to say that Julie undergoes another conversion. For, remaining faithful to her bookkeeping approach to moral conduct, she rejoices that no reproach can be made to her virtuous conduct. "My love has cost nothing to my innocence," writes Julie in her last letter, and we sense that only because she can say this much can she also allow herself to take pleasure in reminiscing about her feeling for Saint-Preux. On the other hand, her last recollection of her life leaves Julie with the doubt that each stage of her pursuit of virtue—her initial decision to marry Wolmar, her retreat into the Stoic dream of a free interiority, her conversion and her subsequent life at Clarens— amounted in fact to a further step toward the erosion of her sense of identity. Now Julie calls those choices in which she used to take pride "sacrifices" and confesses to herself that to die— the "last sacrifice"—for her really means "only to die once more." She dies serenely, reconciled with her life and hopeful that she will meet Saint-Preux again.

B. THE LIMITS OF AUTONOMY

None of the characters of *The New Heloise* is a direct embodiment of an ethic of authenticity. Saint-Preux, Julie, Wolmar and Claire act inauthentically most of the time, quite often deceive themselves about their true motives and even try to deceive one another.[23] Yet this novel still possesses a relevance for us insofar as it highlights the potential for repression inherent in an autonomous moral conscience not complemented by sensitivity to the equilibrium of identity and by authenticity.

One interpretation of *The New Heloise* that held sway for a long time portrayed it as a pre-Romantic restatement of the conflict of virtue versus desire and as a reaffirmation of the morality of "goodheartedness." Babbitt, for example, identifies Rousseau's intention as the glorification of a morality of feeling and depicts Julie as the embodiment of Rousseau's ideal moral character.[24] Neither of these suggestions can be accepted. In fact, all the efforts and selfrepression that the pursuit of virtue costs Julie make her the opposite of a beautiful soul. From her first letter to her lover, Julie emerges more as an example of Sartre's *bad faith* than as the beautiful soul which so many interpreters saw in her.[25] On the other hand, some passages of Rousseau's novel and many of his footnotes support the hypothesis that he neither identified with Julie's moral character nor embraced the moral ideal of the beautiful soul. If anything, he identified more with Saint-Preux.

Another interpretation, first proposed by Kant, locates the significance of the novel in the contrast between, on the one hand, a heteronomous morality of maxims and good feelings and, on the other hand, an autonomous morality of duty. The former view grounds morality in the goodheartedness of the agent and knows of no way to challenge the morality of society. The morality of duty, instead, grounds morality in reason alone and uses a general formal principle, such as the categorical imperative, for passing judgment on the norms of the community. In his interpretation Kant avoids at least one error—namely, he does not equate Julie's notion of moral virtue with the ideal of goodheartedness. However, Kant seems to overlook the ambivalence of Rousseau's attitude toward Julie and again mistakes Julie's approach to morality for Rousseau's.

The significance of the novel has to do, in my opinion, with its touching on the all-modern conflict between an *ethic of autonomy* and an *ethic of authenticity*. Julie is not just caught in the conflict between an "external" norm prescribing obedience to her father's will and the desire to continue her relationship with Saint-Preux. Rather, Julie is caught within a new type of tragic situation, which can be characterized through the notions of sincerity, autonomy and authenticity sketched above. Within her conception of morality her worthiness as a person is defined entirely by moral virtue.[26] From another perspective, of which she has vague glimpses during her conversation with Lord Bomston and during her last moments, Julie realizes that the claims of morality must be balanced with those of identity,[27] but in the end the first view of morality prevails and brings Julie to deny the legitimacy of her sentiment for Saint-Preux in spite of the importance of such a feeling for her identity. Consequently, her attempt to suppress it stifles her sense of self-coherence. Julie becomes a conscientious mother, a faithful wife, a loyal and affectionate friend, a charitable and generous master, but somehow *she* is not quite there in any of these impersonations. Since her acts as a mother, wife and friend do match her feelings, Julie is certainly *sincere* during and after her conversion, but she is not *authentic*. For these feelings and her conduct are the product of intense *emotion-work*, in fact so intense that it has to be partially suppressed from consciousness.

At first sight, the predicament of Julie at the time of her

decision to marry Wolmar appears to be a classical moral dilemma. On one side there is society with its expectations: in this case, Julie is expected to obey her father's will and not endanger her family's reputation. A second aspect of the dilemma is constituted by the force of ethical principles which are independent of those expectations: it is in the name of one of these principles that Julie declines Lord Bomston's offer— namely, the principle which forbids one to pursue one's own happiness at the expense of others. Finally, there is a third side of the dilemma, constituted by the inner world of feelings and emotions which motivate Julie's conduct but also determine her inner needs, and which Julie submits to emotion-work. Whereas emotion-work on behalf of external, social expectations has been considered, since Socrates and Plato, an undignified act and a sign of weakness of character, the emotion work performed at the demand of ethical principles has traditionally been seen as a sign of one's autonomy and strength of character. From the Stoics to Kant, emotion-work on behalf of society's norms has been thought to lead first to the erosion and then to the fragmentation of the self, whereas emotion-work on behalf of one's own moral convictions has been considered not just harmless, but actually conducive to a positive sense of inner strength, vigor and cohesion. In *The New Heloise* Rousseau calls precisely this idea into question. Indirectly, through the vicissitudes of Julie's identity, he suggests that the attempt to master instrumentally one's affective life *always* results in a weakening and eventually in the fragmentation of one's identity, regardless of whether it is carried out on behalf of society's or practical reason's demands. Ironically, for all her inward morality of principle and her consistent application of ethical principles, in the end Julie comes to feel as empty, and as innerly detached from her life, as the Parisian characters described to her by Saint-Preux, whom she self-righteously despises.

Another facet of the contemporary relevance of *The New Heloise* has to do with the contrast of autonomy and authenticity as *ethical* ideals. The dilemma faced by Julie poses the same threat to the coherence of the actor's identity as the one faced by Thomas More in his confrontation with Henry VIII.[28] For both, the integrity or fragmentation of the self is at stake, but the structure of their dilemmas is not identical. More had to choose between two conflicting moral precepts, rooted respectively in the values of loyalty to one's religious convictions and loyalty to a recognized authority. This is a classical tragic situation in that a choice must necessarily be made and there exists no way of satisfying both of the conflicting imperatives. In Julie's case, instead, one horn of the dilemma is constituted by a not-yet-legitimate feeling which contradicts an autonomously chosen principle. This is a new type of tragic situation, not in the sense that people have never before experienced a tension between feelings and conscience, but in the sense that the solution to dilemmas with this structure—traditionally, the subjection of the emotions, passions or inclinations to the priority of ethical norms—has become problematical only in the modern age. We live in a time when it has become fully legitimate to choose one's spouse on a basis other than one's parents preferences. To Julie, however, her love for Saint-Preux, no matter how authentic, cannot appear legitimate without her father's consent and certainly appears to her less morally binding than the duty not to cause the unhappiness of her parents. Rousseau's novel then suggests that sometimes moral choices may have to be made in which the right solution is to side with our feelings, as opposed to our ethical principles, if the feelings in question are bound up with the cohesion of our identity. Such choices are *tragic* in that they presuppose an unsolvable conflict. Yet they are tragic in a *new* sense insofar as we not only may have to act *autonomously* against the moral expectations of our community, but may have also to act *authentically* against our own autonomous principles. Our act would then be justified solely by our considered judgment about the relation of the feeling at issue to our identity.

With the rise of a morality of authenticity a new dimension of bad faith becomes evident. From the standpoint of an ethic of autonomy, bad faith is to pretend that one is acting on one's judgment whereas in fact one is merely following the expectations of others. From the standpoint of an ethic of authenticity, bad faith may concern also our assessment of the relation between feelings and identity. To be in bad faith means to *pretend* that the suppression or containment of a given feeling will affect negatively one's self-cohesion, when in fact only peripheral aspects of our identity will be affected. If we accept the

idea that not all our motives are readily available to our consciousness, then the strict link between all ethics oriented to
authenticity and the pursuit of self-knowledge becomes apparent. In Rousseau's work we can find the suggestion that no true
morality can exist unless one is able to identify the hidden
motives which may influence our conduct and our judgment.
"Our hearts deceive us in a thousand ways," writes Rousseau,
"and act only according to an always secret principle." This
"secret principle" must be thoroughly brought to consciousness, according to Rousseau, before we can act authentically
against a rigid morality of autonomy.

If interpreted along these lines, *The New Heloise* raises a
number of ethical questions to which the contemporary tendencies of our culture have conferred a new relevance. A first set of
questions concerns the foundations and the structure of the
judgment which can suspend the requirements of morality
which endanger our self-identity. Moral actors oriented to
authenticity who wish to identify the aspects of their internal
nature which deserve priority over ethical prescriptions are in
need of guidelines for sorting out the various components of
their identity. Not all that we feel, desire or fear is so ingrained
in our identity as to outweigh the normative cogency of moral
principles. Thus the problem of sorting out the central and the
peripheral elements of an identity leads all ethics of authenticity to attribute a special importance to the faculty of *taste* or to
phronesis.[29] The ethic of autonomy and the ethic of authenticity
appear to presuppose two thoroughly different kinds of universalism. Every ethic of autonomy grounds its appraisal of the
moral valence of an action on some ethical "first principle"—
for instance, the categorical imperative, one's dedication to pro-
fessional achievement, progress in history, or the greatest happiness for the greatest number—and justifies such a principle
by some kind of rational argument proceeding from self-evi-
dence, "analytical truths," or basic intuitions. In this view, initially formulated by Kant but still propounded today by Rawls
and Habermas, judgment, taste or *phronesis* enter the ethical
picture only when the general principle has to be *applied* to
some concrete context of choice. To put it in Kantian terms, the
determination of what is right to do in a given situation is
understood by all ethics of autonomy according to the model of

determinant judgment—i.e., as the *subsumption* of the concrete facts of the matter under the heading of an already existing universal. The categories of "right" and "wrong" already possess their meaning prior to and independently of the facts of the matter upon which judgment has to be passed. On the contrary, all ethics of authenticity take distance from this model and tend, in one vocabulary or other, to conceive of the attribution of the ethical predicate "right" after the model of *reflective* judgment. Within this model, the principle in light of which the projected course of action can be understood does not exist separately from the context of action, but rather has to be identified simultaneously with the identification of the facts of the matter to which the principle is relevant. The absence of a *general* principle, however, does not undermine the universalistic valence of the claims raised by an ethic of authenticity. It only affects the *demonstrability* of those claims. Like the judgment on the wellformedness of a work of art, which operates in the absence of an *a-priori* principle of beauty but can nonetheless assess the degree of well-formedness of single works of art relative to one another and claim universality for such appraisals, also the ethical judgment framed within an ethic of authenticity, for all its renouncing a general principle abstracted from all contexts and its understanding "what is right to do" as "what is right *for me* to do," does not thereby renounce universalism. Its *sui generis* universalism lies in the fact that while the determination of who we are and what best suits our identity cannot exclude reference to our self-understanding and our preferences, at the same time it is not something of which we are the only and final arbiters. Evidence of this lies in the fact that about this nexus—the relation between who we are and the authenticity of a given choice for us—there can be *debate* in a way that there cannot be with regard to our internal states or preferences, which are at most the object of first person reports. To Luther's claim "I can do no other," one can always reply "I'm not sure." That is, both our understanding of who we are and our opinion on the adequacy of a certain view of moral rightness to our constitutive project can be disputed. The universalist valence of prudential or reflective-judgment notions of ethical rightness, singular and undemonstrable as the universalistic valence of aesthetic judgment for Kant, consists in the fact that in claiming the adequacy of a certain notion of rightness for us, we implicitly claim that all those who know enough about who we are and have some intuitive idea of morality *ought* to agree. The singularity of such judgment, a consequence of which is the fact that the rightness of a certain view of morality holds only for us, subtracts nothing from the strong normativity which such judgment commands both among us and among those who know enough about us.

A second set of questions raised by the ethic of authenticity concerns the relation between intimacy and the exercise of moral judgment. Intimate relations provide the optimal terrain for developing an understanding of one's motives, but the wholesome acceptance of the other's identity that they require makes the exercise of moral judgment more problematical. Ultimately morality—even a morality of authenticity—must retain a normative thrust, a trace of the *Sollen*, and for this reason is bound to clash, in one way or other, with the requirement, embedded in all intimate relations, that we bracket all *a-priori* normativity and unconditionally accept "the existent" in the form of the inner reality of the other person.[30]

Finally, a third set of questions linked with the ethic of authenticity regards the cultural tension, typical of contemporary culture, between two notions of the self which presuppose different attitudes toward the normative demands of society. On one hand, we find in today's culture the notion of a self whose worthiness consists in recognizing its own mark in all action, in refusing to obey rules that no longer meet its inner needs or to honor agreements that stifle its development, and in refusing to anchor its identity in the continuity of life-long commitments. On the other hand, we find the notion of a self whose worthiness rests on respecting the norms and abiding by freely entered obligations *especially* when they come at odds with its inclinations. This type of self defines inner strength and worth in terms of sacrifice, self-abnegation, renunciation of satisfaction in the name of higher ideals.[31] In our times we all more or less partake of these ideal types of personal identity, but no one has yet found a way to integrate them. There is no Golden Mean between fulfilment and commitment, nor can an equidistant point be found between obedience and disobedience, compliance with normative claims and their infringement. Until a true mediation between these two modalities of the modern identity emerges, our culture will continue to waver between, on the one hand, the temptation to disentangle the self from all commitments and binding choices, to make it resist all attachments and go through all sorts of changes without being fundamentally changed and, on the other hand, the temptation to follow the reassuring, familiar path of a morality of self-abnegation, of the dedication to commitments, values, and mores which *define*, rather than *express*, our subjectivity.

These questions are *our* questions, which emerge in the reflections of today's social theory and philosophy. Although they transcend the horizon of the ethical problems which concerned Rousseau and his contemporaries, these questions remain rooted in that horizon in a sense which I will try to explicate in the rest of this work.

6

ETHICS AND THE TENSIONS OF MODERNITY:
A NEOWEBERIAN INTERPRETATION

We are now at the end of our journey through Rousseau's social and ethical thought. In the preceding chapters we have looked at four of his major works and have focused on his critique of the modern form of social reproduction, his theory of political right, his implicit psychology and his ethic of authenticity. Above I have claimed that the relevance of some of Rousseau's central themes, especially of his implicit ethic of authenticity, transcends the boundaries of the historical situation of his times and of the mere history of ideas. In the remainder of this essay I would like to make explicit the terms of this significance.

Rousseau's social and ethical thought still speaks to contemporary issues in two basic senses. First, it undermines in at

111

least one important respect the neoconservative interpretation of contemporary culture. Second, it constitutes a balanced response to cultural tensions which arose at the onset of the modern age and which only today have unfolded in their entirety. I will discuss first the relevance of Rousseau for a critique of neoconservatism and then his contribution to the development of Western ethics.

A. ROUSSEAU AND THE POSTMODERN SYNDROME

The main themes of Rousseau's work, according to the reconstruction outlined above, strike a dissonant note against the neoconservative interpretation of contemporary modernity. The neoconservatives characterize our time as a time in which the culture—both high and popular—of the advanced industrial societies is rapidly parting ways with the tradition of Western rationalism. According to their analyses several diverse phenomena are linked together in a sort of postmodern syndrome. Among the phenomena in which the irrationalist *Zeitgeist* of the late twentieth century would manifest itself, the neoconservatives include the widespread disenchantment with the competitive ways of economic and social modernity, the equally widespread disenchantment with the Puritan equation of self-realization and vocational achievement, the tendency to replace this view with a new equation of selfrealization and personal growth, the disaffection with politics as a strategic game, the increasing distrust of the universalistic claims of science and morality and, finally, the increasing emphasis put on intimacy as an intrinsically rewarding experience. These trends are presented as new, as recent, and as amounting to a radical subversion of the rationalist bent of Western culture. From a causal point of view, the emergence of the postmodern syndrome is attributed by the neoconservatives to the influence of aesthetic modernism, either in its artistic-bohemian form or in its therapeutic version.

For all the ambiguity of some of his political views and the doubtfulness of some of his polemical goals, the case of Rousseau cannot be easily fitted into this picture. Many elements of the postmodern syndrome are, however, present in his work. For example, Rousseau frames his critique of the modern form of social reproduction from the standpoint of the effects of competition on interpersonal relations and self-identity. Against these effects of modern civil society Rousseau invokes the image of social relations liberated from the pressure of strategic modes of conduct. These social relations he sees anticipated, before the establishment of a just institutional order, in the attainment of undistorted intimate relations. Intimate relations free of strategic motives, in turn, are considered by Rousseau a fertile terrain for the growth of that mature moral conscience, capable of complementing autonomy with authenticity, which represents an indispensable ingredient of significant and durable social change. Finally, Rousseau's remedy for the erosion of autonomous subjectivity caused by a competitive civil society calls not for learning more effective ways of controlling one's inner world but for a more accepting attitude toward the real self, not for more self-abnegation but for more self-realization.

On the other hand, Rousseau can hardly be mistaken for an advocate of aesthetic modernism. Not only is he not a precursor of the outlook which Bell and the others ascribe to Baudelaire, but, on the contrary, Rousseau can arguably be considered an *adversary* of aesthetic modernism. If anything, Rousseau sided with the Puritan dislike for play. Always distrustful of the arts, he opposed the construction of a theater in Geneva on the ground that the stage would inevitably breed vanity and corruption among the people. Accustomed to the ways of the city, Rousseau incessantly contrasted their decadent sophistication with what he idealized as the simple and straightforward manners of the countryside. Finally, though deeply influenced by the French culture and intellectuals of his times, Rousseau continued to extol the "lack of affectation" of Swiss culture. To sum up, one need not share Rousseau's puritanical biases to realize that his case does not corroborate the neoconservative hypothesis of an elective affinity, let alone of a causal link, between the ideology of making of one's life a work of art typical of the aesthetic avant-garde and the emphasis on authenticity typical of contemporary modernity. In fact, in Rousseau we can find a powerful anticipation of the former coupled with a very strong aversion to the latter.

However, the significance of Rousseau's social and ethical thought goes beyond its constituting a piece of counterevidence

against the plausibility of the neoconservative thesis on contemporary modernity. If so many assonances with contemporary themes can be found in Rousseau it is because Rousseau
was able, as a perceptive observer of his times, to sense two
cultural tensions of a new kind, opened by the rise and affirmation of the Protestant ethos over against the ethos of brotherliness typical of premodern Christianity. The cultural trends of
today's culture by and large represent responses, belated and
not yet definitive, to the same *moral* tensions of cultural modernity. In this sense, these trends represent no subversion of the
developmental path of Western culture, but on the contrary
contain many aspects of continuity with the evolution of Western ethics. Although so evident to Rousseau, who wrote when
the formation of these tensions was still in its beginnings, the
ethical, as opposed to *aesthetical*, basis of his and today's emphasis on authenticity still escapes the neoconservatives' comprehension. In a sense, the very idea of a tension between an *aesthetically* motivated and an *ethically* motivated emphasis on
authenticity requires a word of explanation. Different versions
of the concept of authenticity are shaping contemporary culture, much in the same way as different versions of the concept
of autonomy—as diverse, for instance, as the notions of autonomy to be found in the works of Locke, Voltaire, Kant, Fichte,
Schelling or Hegel—shaped the modern consciousness. The
aesthetic and the ethic versions of the concept of authenticity
have in common an aversion against the reason-centered
notion of subjectivity typical of the Western tradition from
Socrates to the Enlightenment—i.e., the view of human subjectivity as split between a higher, rational nature, and the "lower"
nature of the emotions, and the related understanding of the
good life as the domination and mastery of the world of emotions by the rational side of the human self. While "Know thy-
self" has been the *leitmotif* of this vision for centuries, contemporary modernity begins when at the center of Western
sensibility a new *leitmotif*, for which no individual Socrates can
be credited, is enthroned—"Know the other." Perhaps the first
occurrence of this new, contemporary-modern, attitude is given
by Wittgenstein's remark that Frazer, the author of *The Golden
Bough*, is more of a savage than most of the savages whom he
describes.[1] The aesthetic and the ethic versions of the notion of

authenticity, however, part ways in other respects. First, while the emphasis on authenticity typical of the aesthetic avantgarde and partially of Nietzsche regards the attainment of authenticity exclusively, and reductively, as the breaking free of an imprisoned subjectivity from the bonds of existing normativity—thus viewing norms, institutions, and roles only in a negative way, as constraining the expression of subjectivity—the ethical conception of authenticity includes the realization that norms, roles and institutions also *sustain* subjectivity.

Second, the aesthetic approach to authenticity, being centered around the category of the sublime, views as suspicious all attempts to bring self-experience to a synthesis. The good life seems then to coincide with noncumulative openness, with letting oneself drift across an irreducible multiplicity of particular experiences, and with the wandering of the nomad. The ethical version of authenticity distances itself from this view. While the authentic self is not made to coincide with any "rational core," as in the ethic of autonomy, and while one's deviations from one's ideal self are taken to be as representative of who one is as one's conscious ideals, at the same time all ethical approaches to authenticity refuse to reduce self-realization to drifting with the tide of contingent and peripheral experiences. The notion of a design, even in the weakest form of an ex-post-facto attempt to attribute the order of a *narrative* to the contingent episodes of one's life remains crucial, though of course, unlike an ethic of autonomy, ethical conceptions of authenticity understand the core of the self as related to what is unique to a single individual and not to what, within each individual, is common to everybody.

Third, the two notions of authenticity incorporate a radically different attitude towards the differentiation of value spheres and the consequent decentering of reason which characterizes cultural modernity. Aesthethic-oriented views, from Schlegel to Novalis, from Baudelaire to the surrealists, from Nietzsche to Derrida, not only understand the aesthetic sphere as the antagonist of rationality, but they also see it as the *only locus of meaning*. The paradigmatic act of rebelling against the constraints of existing normativity is understood as defining the only truly meaningful horizon of meaning. Action inspired by other value-spheres, for example action motivated by the quest for truth or by the moral point of view, is then devalued to the semblance of action, to the manipulatory or self-deluding manifestation of something deeper, a drive for self-assertion, the will to power, the desire for dominating the other, and the like. In a sense, the view of authenticity implicit in the aesthetic avantgarde is but the latest, and perhaps the last, of the compensatory monotheisms to which the erosion of the integrative power of traditional religious worldviews has given rise. Like Comte's and Spencer's positivist emphasis on the scientific attitude as the only meaningful way of relating to the world, or Marx's view of revolutionary politics as the sphere of action which would give meaning to all other spheres of action, or Hegel's view of philosophical reflection as capable of exercising the integrative function which used to belong to religion, so *aesthetic modernism* singles out the realm of aesthetically motivated conduct as the only authentic conduct—i.e., as the only type of conduct capable of having meaning in its own right instead of constituting a distorted reflection of the will to power, of resentment or of something else. The ethically based notions of authenticity, instead, view authentic action as action in which the various moments of modern rationality are *all* somehow reflected. *Balance* is here the key word. Schiller's notions of play and of the beautiful soul come to mind, along with their contemporary equivalent: the psychoanalytic view of a good identity and especially Winnicott's view of "creative living."[2] Schiller's ideal of a personality endowed with *grace and dignity*, or with authenticity in an ethical sense, is best illustrated by his analogy between inner life and polity. We do not call 'liberal,' argues Schiller—using the term 'liberal' in the same generic sense of praise that we often associate with the term 'democratic'—a society where the sovereign asserts his will against that of the citizens or the citizens assert their will against that of the sovereign. For in the first case the government would be despotic and in the second no government at all would exist. We only call a society 'liberal' in which, although every decision proceeds from one and the same will, the citizen believes that he lives in freedom and obeys only his own disposition.[3] Similarly, we understand authentic subjectivity or, in Schiller's terms, a beautiful soul endowed with grace and dignity, as one which neither dissolves its unity into the plurality of inclinations (as the postmodernist advocates of the centerless self would have us do) nor suppresses those feelings and emotions that fail to pass the test of our moral principles (like the proponents of the ethic of autonomy urge everyone to do, even at the cost of thereby generating a moral character which possesses dignity but lacks grace), but as subjectivity which is able to integrate its different constitutive moments—i.e., its feelings, and its cognitive and moral rationality—or, in Schiller's words, to "obey reason with joy."[4] Authenticity with an ethical accent entails the balanced rearticulation—without dedifferentiation—of the moments of rationality that modernity has differentiated. Authenticity with an aesthetic accent, instead, connects what Kierkegaard called the "aesthetic life" with a certain ontology of the centerless self and claims that the form of life resulting from such combination is the only one ultimately fit for the contemporary self.

Returning to Rousseau, we suggest that the significance of his work in the evolution of modern ethics is not as immediately evident as its relevance in anticipating contemporary themes of authenticity, self-realization and intimacy, but it requires that we reconstruct briefly the cultural context to which the ethic of authenticity implicit in Rousseau makes an original contribution. This context is constituted by the evolution of Western ethics in the modern age after the affirmation of the Puritan ethic.

B. WEBER'S CONCEPTION OF ETHICAL EVOLUTION AS RATIONALIZATION

To evaluate the contribution made by Rousseau's thought to the development of modern Western ethics requires that we outline a general framework for making sense of the development of Western ethics and of the notion of a contribution to it. This framework can by and large be derived from Max Weber's work. The aspect of Weber's legacy most directly relevant for understanding today's cultural tendencies can be found not so much in the prophecy of the "iron cage" at the end of *The Protestant Ethic*, which has inspired the analyses of the neoconservatives, as in the parts of *Economy and Society* where Weber reconstructs not so much the history of ethical thought as the *evolution* or, in his words, the process of *rationalization*, under-gone by Western ethics from its beginnings to the Puritan ethos.[5] In those pages Weber is directly concerned with the pro-grammatic question which underlies not only *The Protestant Ethic*, but the whole of his *Gesammelte Aufsätze zur Religionssozi-ologie*, namely why in the West, and in the West only, "cultural phenomena have appeared which (as we like to think) lie in a line of development having *universal* significance and value."[6] These phenomena can be summed up in the peculiarly rational-ist mentality which manifests itself in almost every product of our culture, from science to musical notation, from architecture to bureaucracy, from the capitalist enterprise to the legal form of domination typical of the modern state. The answer to this question is found by Weber in the potential for the rationaliza-tion of one's conduct of life inherent in some typical ingredients of Western religiosity, such as the prevalence of ethical over exemplary prophecy, the prevalence of a notion of the divinity as a source of ethical law rather than as an immanent cosmic principle, a strong disposition toward monotheism, the tenden-cy to understand evil as a principle opposed to the divinity, and the prevalence of 'ascetic', as opposed to mystical, ways of seeking salvation. The presence of these cultural ingredients in the Western religions has contributed, according to Weber, to an increasing rationalization of ethical thought and religious doc-trines in the first place, and of all aspects of everyday life in the second. I will not discuss here Weber's thesis concerning the causal contribution offered by this process of rationalization, culminating in the Puritan ethos, to the rise of capitalism. Rather, it is more important for our theme to briefly highlight four presuppositions which underlie Weber's approach to cul-tural evolution.

The first presupposition concerns the notion of rationaliza-tion used by Weber in his investigations in the development of religious ideas and Western culture. In the context of these studies the term *rationalization* has little to do with the idea of a prevalence of instrumental considerations within social action or of an accrued interest in the optimization of means to ends. Just as little has the notion of cultural rationalization to do with the idea of calculability which Weber often associates with the rationality of social conduct. Rather, for a culture, a religion or a life-style to undergo rationalization means to make as explicit as possible the whole of its value assumptions and to render this whole as coherent as possible. For Weber a system of meanings—for example, a world-view, a religious ethic, a cosmology, or a theological doctrine—is rational to the extent that its underlying premises are explicit and consistent.[7]

The second presupposition specifies the meaning of rationalization for the area of religion proper. For a historical religion to undergo rationalization means to render explicit and consistent its way of addressing the anthropological constants of suffering, of death and of the discrepancy between merit and fortune. All religious ethics must provide an explication of the meaning of these common human experiences. The internal evolution of ethics, for Weber, consists in making this explication more and more articulate and consistent. The motor of this process of rationalization is constituted by the presence, and the continuous reproduction at a higher level, of ambiguities, tensions and outright contradictions.

Of course, an investigation of its internal rationalization can tell us little about the historical influence of a given religion or ethics. This is Weber's third presupposition. The concrete social effects of the rationalization of a given religious doctrine or of a form of morality mostly depend on the constellation of interests which its diffusion can mobilize, legitimate or simply hurt. In this sense, a doctrine or moral view which from a strictly evolutionary standpoint constitutes an advance may actually remain historically ineffectual if it fails to attract the attention of concrete and relevant social groups, whereas it may release momentous social transformations when it gives voice, as in the case of Calvinism, to the needs and identity of rising social groups.

The fourth presupposition underlying Weber's approach to the evolution of culture concerns a programmatic rather than substantive point. In his studies of the religious basis of Western rationalism Weber chooses a course which allows him to steer clear of two risks which have run aground several attempts similar to his. Weber manages to avoid both the abstractness of a typological comparison of various religious cultures and the risk of falling into a sort of teleological evolutionism. Instead of characterizing the specificity of Western rationalism merely through a static comparison of its differences and similarities with an ideal-typical Eastern religiosity, Weber characterizes the specificity of his object of inquiry through a reconstruction of the "developmental history" of Western religiosity. We encounter here, in *Economy and Society*, an unusually Hegelian Weber, for whom to understand the specificity of modern Western rationalism means, as it did for Hegel, to understand its genesis and internal development. Yet Weber parts ways with Hegel insofar as he does not claim necessity for the evolutionary sequences that he reconstructs. Whereas the question underlying Hegel's reconstruction of various cultural transformations in *The Phenomenology of Spirit* is usually "Why does y necessarily follow from x?", Weber's question is always of the form "How is it possible that from x followed y?". Weber does not set out to explain why Catholicism *should* give rise to a more rational religion, such as Calvinism, but tries to explain how Calvinism, with its emphasis on rational 'asceticism', *could* possibly arise out of medieval Catholicism.

Finally, in his *Religionssoziologie*, unlike in his methodological essays, often Weber insists on the overall superiority of one ethical system or one religious culture over another. The problem is, however, that when he maintains that a religious ethic of norms provides an answer to the fundamental questions of human existence superior to, or more rational than, the answer provided by a magical religiosity, or when he suggests that an ethic of conviction, such as the Puritan ethic, constitutes an advance over the ethic of medieval Catholicism, Weber usually justifies these judgments with reference to the substantive aspects of the cultural forms at issue, but tells us nothing about the criteria underlying his contention. This set of criteria implicit in Weber's theory of cultural rationalization must be made explicit through the work of interpretation.

Following W. Schluchter, we can generate the set of implicit criteria underlying Weber's analysis by integrating the Weberian typology of religious ethics with Kohlberg's theory of moral development.[8] According to Kohlberg, the moral development of the individual goes through three main levels.[9] At the first level, which Kohlberg calls *preconventional*, an action is judged morally good if it can generate pleasure for the actor and can satisfy the actor's needs or occasionally those of others. At the next level, called the *conventional* level, an action counts as morally good if it intentionally meets the expectations of a higher authority or reference group, for example of God, of the king, or of the elders, the priests, the clan. Finally, at the *postconventional* stage, an action is considered good insofar as its consequences or its underlying intention (or both) are in agreement with a general principle chosen autonomously by the moral actor on the basis of its qualities of consistency, universal applicability and comprehensiveness.[10] From these three stages of the individual moral conscience it is possible to abstract four criteria for the assessment of ethical doctrines and moral cultures in terms of their degree of ethical evolution. More specifically, we can distinguish ethical doctrines and moral cultures according to:

1. The *domain* of validity of moral judgment.

2. The *foundations* of the validity of moral judgment.

3. The *nature of the object* of moral judgment.

4. The *type of consciousness* presupposed.

The *domain* of validity of an ethical system regards the definition of who is bound by the moral judgments and prescriptions generated within the system. The domain may be restricted to a particular set of actors, such as the clan or the tribe, or may extend to larger group, or the entire human species. From this standpoint, ethical evolution proceeds toward an increasing *universalism*.

The *foundations* of moral judgment concern the conditions under which an act of moral justification is considered valid and binding. When the foundations of the validity of moral judgment undergo a transformation, as it was the case with the rise of modernity, it is not just that one or the other single justification is no longer regarded as valid, but rather that a certain *kind* of justification is no longer considered compelling. For example, at the preconventional level an action is right because it can produce pleasurable consequences or, at the conventional level, because it agrees with the norms of the community. At the post-conventional level an action is right if it does not contradict certain formal principles of reciprocity. From this second standpoint, ethical evolution proceeds from concreteness to abstractness and from immediacy to *reflexivity*. The more developed a moral culture, the wider the gap between the everyday, concrete terms in which a dilemma first arises and the abstract terms in which its solution can be formulated. Furthermore, the more developed a moral culture, the higher the degree of reflexivity. At the most primitive levels of moral conscience only isolated actions can be evaluated in ethical terms, then at the conventional level the rightness of entire classes of actions can be assessed on the basis of norms, and at the post-conventional level we can evaluate the rightness of norms with reference to principles. Finally, at a stage of reflexivity which up to now has remained the exclusive domain of philosophy, it is possible to evaluate the appropriateness of moral principles.

The *object* of valuation also varies in accordance with the degree of evolution. From this third standpoint, ethical doctrines and moral cultures evolve along a dimension of *complexity*, from a level at which primarily single acts are put under scrutiny to levels where ethical assessment concerns the conduct of an entire lifetime.

Finally, the various types of ethics presuppose different levels of minimal cognitive ability. At the early stages of evolution this minimal competence includes merely the ability to tell *is* from *ought*, but an ethic of principles such as the Puritan ethos requires autonomy and an ethic of responsibility, such as that advocated by Weber, requires also a quality of flexibility. From this last standpoint, ethics evolve toward an increasing *individuation*.

If we combine these four standpoints, we can understand Weber's notion of ethical rationalization as an evolutionary process which results in an increasing autonomy of the individual from external authorities and communal symbols, in an increasing abstractness of moral prescriptions, in an increasing complexity of the object of moral judgment and, finally, in extending the bindingness of moral prescriptions to all human beings.

C. THE TENSIONS OF MODERN MORALITY

We are now in a position to reconstruct the main aspects of the evolutionary process which has given rise to those modern moral tensions against which the significance of Rousseau's ethical thought can be appraised. The first turning point is constituted by the transition from a *magical ethic* to a *religious ethic of norms*, the second by the transition to an *ethic of principle* and the third by the new cultural context determined by the diffusion of the Puritan ethos. I will touch only cursorily on the first two turning points and will focus more on the third.

The term *magical ethics*, strictly speaking, is misleading, in that at this stage of ethical evolution no norms exist, no consciousness of wrongdoing, nor any notion of guilt or sin. The moral evaluation of action concerns only the objective consequences and not the actor's intention. Prescriptions regard single actions and only occasionally, in the form of magical taboos, classes of actions. The world-view typical of this stage of ethical evolution is monistic. In fact, although magical thought admits of a kind of 'double world', i.e. the realm of ordinary things and events and the 'world behind the world' inhabited by demons and deities, there is no clearcut separation between the two. The world is still the 'enchanted garden' in which all natural processes possess some form of meaning. The spirits who inhabit the enchanted garden do not yet possess an autonomous will. Thus men do not need to address them through prayers or supplications. For these spirits can be coerced by men through the skillful execution of magical manipulations over certain symbolic objects. In this sense, points out Weber, they are inferior and not superior to man.

The world-view embedded in magic interprets the discrepancy between fortune and merit as the product of malevolent spirits who have been angered, intentionally or unintentionally, by one's misconceived magical acts. Insofar as we can speak of an *ethical* evaluation, a magical ethic conceives rightness or wrongness only as the property of *single* actions—single actions considered merely under the aspect of their actual consequences and not of their underlying intention. The type of consciousness required of the moral actor in order to operate at this stage is still heteronomous and quite undifferentiated. The actor must be able to appraise the immediate consequences of action, to carry out a certain measure of strategic calculation and to recognize the social and natural contexts to which the relevant taboos apply. Since moral rightness is still fused with magical efficacy, the actor knows of no conflict between duty and inclination.

A major evolutionary advance occurs with the rise of a *religious ethic of norms*.[11] Whereas in magical ethics no religious or divine law existed, with the transition to a religious ethic of norms the demons are transformed into gods whose will can no longer be coerced through magical manipulation, but is the source of moral prescriptions binding for *all* the members of the community.[12] This shift toward a higher degree of universalism is accompanied by a new differentiation. It becomes possible for the moral actor to distinguish between moral guilt and the unpleasant consequences of action. Any infringement of divine will becomes a wrong action regardless of its results. At this stage "goodness is then envisaged as an integral capacity for an attitude of holiness, and for consistent behavior derived from such an attitude."[13] This "attitude of holiness" is no longer defined by compliance with isolated taboos, but by obedience to sets of *norms*. The Ten Commandments are one such body of substantive norms, whose observance can ensure ethical compensation. Compensation for suffering, when suffering is interpreted in the light of sin and God's will to punish the transgressors of His law, takes the form of *salvation* along with rebirth—i.e. it takes the form of permanently enjoying the favor of the gods. The horror of punishment and the conditions for attaining salvation are no longer spelled out in the form of mythical narratives. Rather, they take the form of *doctrines* elaborated by priests and other officials. The object of ethical evaluation becomes more complex in that religious norms now govern entire classes of actions, considered also from the standpoint of the actor's intention and not merely from that of their objective consequences. The ground for the validity of moral judgment shifts from magical or technical success to adherence to the revealed norms and an autonomous realm of morality is thereby constituted. Finally, the type of competence necessary for operating within an ethic of norms is more complex. The moral actor remains characterized by heteronomy— he or she is never required to pass judgment on the community's mores, let alone on the norms given by God—but now must be able to separate questions of utility from questions of rightness, to subsume acts under the correct class of permitted or prohibited actions, and to control his or her passions more strictly. It is at this stage of moral evolution that the conflict between moral reason and the passions becomes a theme for ethical reflection.

The transition from the ethic of concrete norms to an *ethic of principle*, stimulated in the West by the Puritan ethos, inaugurates the modern form of morality. Calvin's ethics, if considered from the perspective outlined above, contains several important advances over the premodern ethic of norms. First, the basis of moral justification and judgment undergoes a quantum leap along the dimension of reflexivity. Human conduct is deemed right no longer on the basis of whether it complies with substantive norms such as the Ten Commandments, but rather on the basis of its satisfying an overarching ethical principle—in the case of Puritanism, the duty to further God's plan through dedication to one's calling. Furthermore, not only conduct but also the religious norms themselves can be evaluated in terms of their fitting the principle of vocational achievement. This principle, however, is still taken by the Puritan as a godly command never to be questioned. In this sense Puritanism represented only the *starting point* of the rationalization of ethics in the modern age. The Kantian ethics constituted a further step along this path, in that the categorical imperative is no longer a principle legitimated through divine will, but is understood as a necessary presupposition of practical reason.

Second, with the Puritan ethos the complexity of the object of valuation increases. Moral judgment is no longer a matter of primarily assessing whether a certain action is right in and of itself. Up to medieval Catholicism merit or demerit for salvation was linked with the concrete intent underlying each single action. Consequently, points out Weber, the conduct of life remained, from the viewpoint of ethics, "an unmethodical and miscellaneous succession of discrete actions."[14] The radical innovation introduced into the methodology of salvation by the Protestant sects, and especially by Calvinism, consisted of treating individual actions and "good works" as manifestations of an underlying global disposition of the personality. On the one hand, actions whose outcome is good out of lucky circumstances no longer add up to one's religious merits and, on the other hand, actions that stem from atypical and extraordinary motivations not rooted in the personality are also devalued. To muster all of one's inner resources in order to redeem a life of cowardice through an act of extraordinary courage becomes, from the Puritan standpoint, less meritorious than to perform less extraordinary actions out of a habitual inclination toward bravery. Then the best way of achieving salvation becomes the relentless training of one's character for the purpose of achieving a "rationalized methodical direction of the entire pattern of life."[15] Consequently, moral judgment becomes a matter of evaluating conduct in terms of its reflecting an overall pattern of life as well as of judging that pattern of life in relation to the principle of the dedication to one's calling. Again, Calvin's ethic represents in this respect only the starting point of the evolution of modern Western morality. For the conduct of one's life is evaluated only from the standpoint of its underlying *intention*—which is why the Puritan ethic remains an *ethic of conviction* or an *ethic of ultimate ends*. A further development will be constituted by the *ethics of responsibility*, including Weber's own version, which extend the evaluation to the foreseeable *consequences* of a certain conduct of life. Third, differently that all the preceding forms of ethics, an ethic of principle such as the Puritan presupposes moral actors endowed with autonomy.

However, the features of the Puritan ethic which contributed to create the cultural tensions reflected in Rousseau's social and ethical thought have to do not only with these formal advances, but also with the substantive influence of Calvin's ethic on the cultural situation of early modernity. The Puritan ethic represented an innovative solution to the cultural tensions that arose from the clash between the traditional ethos of brotherliness and the motivations required by the incipient modernization of the economic and political relations. Yet the solution provided by Calvinism created *new* tensions which, magnified by the subsequent institutionalization of many aspects of the Puritan ethos, form the background against which many of our contemporary trends must be understood.

In "Religious Rejections of the World and their Directions,"[16] Weber focuses on the tensions that arose, during the early stages of modernity, between the process of rationalization undergone by six distinct spheres of social action and the ethos of brotherliness inherent in premodern religiosity. First Weber considers the economic sphere. The ethos underlying most of the premodern religions, including medieval Catholicism, was an ethos of immediate solidarity and mutual support between all the members of a community based on the principle: "your want of today may be mine of tomorrow."[17] Such a principle could not but enter a collision course with the motivational imperatives of a modernizing economy. In fact, the systematic pursuit of wealth through the rational organization of the enterprise and the rational management of all resources, including human labor, rested on the motivational viability and the cultural acceptability of a new kind of social relations based on pure economic interest—the *cash nexus*. Within these social relations there is no place for the 'brother', but there are only 'others'. In the early and mid sixteenth century, due to a process of capitalist accumulation already under way, to the generalized flourishing of mercantile activities and to the expansion of manufacturing ventures in England and to some extent in Continental Europe, this emerging sector of the economy, still submerged by the more traditional economic relations, began to seriously challenge the ideal of brotherhood embedded in traditional Catholicism. At this point in the history of Western culture, according to Weber, only two ways of reconciling this antagonism remained open. One was a mystic flight from the world in the form of an objectless devotion to everybody not for man's sake but for devotion's sake.[18] The other solution consisted in the renunciation of the command to love others as 'brothers'. The latter was the solution embraced by Puritanism. Calvinist theology legitimized, at a time when only a religious legitimation could count, the attitudes of indifference toward suffering which were functional to the further diffusion of the cash nexus.[19]

A similar tension can be found in the sphere of politics. The consolidation of the state at the onset of modernity contributed to the consolidation of the strategic attitudes and modes of conduct best expressed in Machiavelli's thought. These motifs, though present from time immemorial in the practice of the political elites, now began to be sanctioned as the essence of politics. The recognition that the *raison d'état* has a logic of its own quite independent of the sphere of ethics could not but collide with the idea of brotherliness. Also in this case only two paths remained open for a consistent reconciliation of the tension. One was the radically antipolitical attitude of the mystic, the other the Puritan acceptance of the necessity that God's will be imposed "upon the creatural world by the means of this world, namely, violence."[20]

The third sphere of social action considered by Weber is the aesthetic sphere. The relation between art and religion has always been a complex one. Within magical religiosity art had often been used as a means for controlling the gods and, subsequently, art had been used in ancient and Christian civilization for purposes of edification. By and large, a relative harmony had reigned between art and religion as long as the work of art was seen as stemming either either from divine inspiration or from spontaneous play.[21] Instead, as soon as art began to be understood, in the modern age, as an activity oriented toward "consciously grasped independent values which exist in their own right,"[22] a fierce tension arose between art and religion on the terrain of meaning. Both, in fact, purport to offer meaning to people, and above all a kind of meaning which transcends the boundaries of the everyday. To any consistent religion of brotherliness the peculiar salvation from everyday life offered by art is bound to appear, argues Weber, as "irresponsible indulgence and secret lovelessness."[23] In the case of the aesthetic sphere, the devaluation of art inherent in the Puritan strand of the Reformation constituted no special innovation with respect to the more traditional religious attitudes and no stimulus for the further development of a modern culture.

A similar story of early harmony and subsequent tension characterizes the relation between religion and the erotic sphere. Orgiastic practices and sacred prostitution were common ingredients of cult in many premodern religions. Even before the onset of modernity, however, the sphere of love became an autonomous area of conduct with values, rituals and codes of its own. Then to the extent that a culture of eroticism gradually sublimated love into a paramount value and detached it from the naive naturalism of sex, this culture began to clash with the ethic of brotherhood. As in the case of art, a culture of eroticism also requires orientations which often collide with everyday life and again it promises some sort of salvation, this time in the guise of merging with the identity of another, which cannot but appear suspicious to all consistent religion. Also with regard to this sphere of action the Puritan ethos, with its acceptance of an Eros domesticated into marriage-for-procreation, followed the only path open for a coherent rationalization.[24]

The rational pursuit of knowledge constitutes a fifth area of conflict between traditional religiosity and a modernizing society. Every religion must, at some point, demand a sacrifice of the intellect. The pursuit of empirical knowledge through rational methods leads to a 'disenchanted' conception of the world, and any notion of the world as a meaningless causal mechanism cannot but appear threatening to a premodern religious consciousness which takes for granted that the course of the world should be meaningful, at least insofar as human affairs are concerned. Calvinism responded to this tension as all its predecessors did, namely with a devaluation of nonrevealed knowledge, but introduced an important distinction. The depreciation of, and distrust of, human knowledge concerned only the attempt to grasp the totality of the world through metaphysical or philosophical categories, and never affected the rational pursuit of knowledge through empirical research, especially in the field of the natural sciences.

Finally, a sixth area of cultural tensions had to do with the problem of theodicy. Early Christianity and Catholicism considered the devil as the source of evil and at the same time as a creature of God, albeit degenerate. This solution was inconsistent, in that the assumption of God's omniscience and omnipotence was difficult to reconcile in this case with the presupposition of a fatherly and loving God. Calvinism abandoned the idea of God's fatherly benevolence altogether and thereby eliminated the inconsistency.

In the analysis outlined above is contained the most interesting indication that Weber can offer for the study of the cultural transformations connected with contemporary modernity. Weber located the significance of Protestantism for the development of Western culture in its embodying a better, in the sense of more consistent, set of responses to the tensions of early modernity than its more traditional predecessors or, to use his terminology, in Puritanism's superior potential for the rationalization of Western ethics. The same research strategy can be applied to the context subsequent to the affirmation of Puritanism. If it is not implausible that the Puritan solution to the tensions of early modernity, beside contributing to the process of modernization investigated by Weber, also opened new tensions in the sphere of morality, then it makes sense to look at the further developments of Western ethics—developments that the secularization of society shifted from a religious to a primarily philosophical plane—from the standpoint of their containing diverse and sometimes competing solutions to these new tensions. From this perspective, Weberian yet alternative to the neoconservative approach, one can evaluate the potential for rationalization inherent in various modern philosophical traditions and in the contemporary by-products of such positions at the level of popular consciousness. In contrast to the approach adopted by Bell and the others, this perspective does not blind one to the positive aspects of today's culture. To be sure, I cannot offer here a complete reconstruction of the post-Protestant tensions of cultural modernity or an assessment of the competing solutions elaborated by Western culture during the last two centuries, nor can I investigate the social factors which to various degrees promote the new ethical views among the social groups of the advanced industrial societies. Rather, I will briefly describe two of the moral tensions opened by the affirmation of the Puritan ethic and will then discuss the response to them implicit in the ethical thought of Rousseau.

The new cultural tensions created by the Calvinist solution to the clash between the motivational requisites of a modernizing society and the premodern ethos of brotherliness can be grouped, as far as the sphere of morality is concerned, into two basic types: *formal* and *substantive* tensions.

On the one hand there are tensions rooted in the *formal* properties of the Puritan ethic. Just by virtue of being the first *ethic of principle* to be widely diffused and institutionalized in the West, Calvinism generated a new kind of cultural tensions. Whereas in all premodern ethics ethical prescriptions are couched in a language, and based on presuppositions, which for the actor maintain the force and indisputability of the contents of primary socialization, at the cultural stage inaugurated by an ethic of principle two modifications occur. First, the mores according to which one has been socialized and which one constantly sees reenacted in the community have lost their privileged status. The realization that they are factually operative does not make them morally justified. Second, abstract principles such as the dedication to one's calling or the categorical imperative contain no specifications as to how they should be applied to concrete cases. In turn, the subsumption of concrete problems under principles so general presupposes cognitive and hermeneutic abilities which were certainly not required of the premodern actor. Furthermore, in contrast with all premodern ethics the courses of action prescribed by a principled ethic often presuppose dispositions and motivations not in line with the basic orientations acquired during primary socialization.[25] The tensions linked with the formal properties of the Puritan ethos can be considered inevitable concomitants of the transition to a modern form of morality. The question arises, however, whether the Puritan ethos did not constitute an exceedingly inhospitable terrain for the growth of those qualities of flexibility and empathy which could have reduced the tensions of ethical modernization to the indispensable minimum or, in other words, whether the fact that cultural modernization took place under the aegis of Puritanism did not entail an unnecessary exacerbation of these unavoidable moral tensions.

On the other hand, some of the moral tensions opened by the hegemonic influence of Calvinism appear to be linked with the *substantive* aspects of the Puritan ethos. Among such tensions we find a *deficit of solidarity* and a *surplus of self-repression*. These tensions, implicit in Weber's account of the social psychology of Protestantism, are rooted not so much in the letter of Calvin's teachings as in the effects of those teachings when popularized in a new code of common sense. The deficit of motivation to social solidarity has its roots in the peculiar position of loneliness which the Puritan conception assigned to the believer. No personal ties, no concrete and individuated love for one's neighbor, no inner disposition toward understanding others and no caring for the other are of any significance for the purpose of one's salvation.[26] Rather, a certain distrust and the determination not to depend on one's neighbor's help were presented by the Puritan preachers as more appropriate qualities in this respect. Reserve and self-reliance were deemed the

attitudes most conducive to success in one's calling and thus to
acquiring the certainty of one's salvation. An excessive sympathy for one's neighbor's suffering, even for the suffering caused
indirectly by one's own success, not only did not help but, insofar as it distracts one from attending the divine plan and dis-
perses one's energies into merely creatural plans for ethical
compensation, could actually hinder one's salvation. In this
sense, the influence of Puritanism went beyond the mere
undermining of the ethos of brotherliness. First congealed into
certain character traits and then institutionalized in the social
roles of the modern societies, the complex of attitudes promoted by Calvinism contributed to the rise of a notion of society as
a mere arena for individual self-assertion. Possessive individualism legitimated a solipsistic posture directed at the mastery of
one's social environment which finds an equivalent in the
species' attempt to master the natural environment. Such an
attitude toward society, in turn, collided not only with an ethos
of brotherliness long since defeated, but also with the orientation toward solidarity required by the integration of the more
complex modern societies.

Alongside a deficit of motivation for solidarity, the Puritan
upbringing produced unprecedented levels of *self-repression*.
The Puritan insistence on a methodical conduct of one's life
translated into an equally systematic repression of those
aspects of the inner world which were not directly connected
with vocational achievement. Ascetic Protestantism condemned sport insofar as it went beyond sheer exercise aimed at
maintaining fitness. Social gatherings, art, and especially the
theater, became all associated with "idle talk" and "ostenta-
tion" and looked upon with suspicion in that they appeared to
depart from the principle of utility.[27] The attempt to discipline
private life and to make it completely instrumental to the certainty of one's salvation went so far, in certain cases, that a cata-
logue of permissible recreational activities was specified,
including: visiting friends, reading historical works, conducting
or watching mathematical and physical experiments, garden-
ing, discussing business and commenting on political events.[28]
In Holland the Calvinist proverb: "You should not eat for the
sake of pleasure" is still remembered today. Yet all these examples barely scratch the surface of the repressive dynamics

inherent in the Puritan socialization. More than a matter of permitted or banned activities, such repression is a matter of the overall relation which the believer is asked to establish between his or her rational will and the inner emotional world. Such a relation takes on the same quality of systematic planning which characterizes the believer's conduct in the social and natural world. The subjective world of affects and emotions becomes a sort of *internal environment*, as it were, which surrounds and limits the exercise of morality as the natural world surrounds and limits the exercise of our instrumental rationality. Since for the Puritan the spontaneous agreement of duty and inclination added little or nothing to the ethical merit of one's conduct, the believer lacked a positive role to assign to affects, feelings and emotions. Affects, emotions and feelings deserve the believer's attention only insofar as they represent a potential source of ethical "trouble" and not because they are constituents of an identity which has to be fulfilled. With this peculiar depreciation of inner nature, however, Calvinism introduced no innovation, but represented merely another way station of Western rationalism, which from Plato to Kant is pervaded by a similar motif. It should be clearer now why the Puritan ethos did not constitute an optimal terrain for the development of the qualities of flexibility, tolerance of ambivalence and of anxiety, self-acceptance, and empathy for the equilibria of identity, which could have attenuated the inevitable tensions of the transition to a modern morality of principle.

7

AUTHENTICITY AND
THE EVOLUTION OF ETHICS

In the last chapter I reconstructed a few aspects of the new cultural context determined by the affirmation of the ascetic strand
of Protestantism as the predominant ethos of Western society.
Within this new context I have paid attention only to the sphere
of morality and, within the sphere of morality, I have focused
on two specific tensions, which I have identified as a deficit of
solidarity and a surplus of self-repression. From this vantage
point the subsequent developments of social and ethical
thought, from the eighteenth century to the present, can be
understood as responses to the modern tensions of morality or,
in Weber's terms, as attempts to further rationalize our moral
culture. Against this background I will discuss once more the
contemporary relevance of Rousseau's ethical views.

135

Let me first summarize what is meant here by the term 'authenticity'. At the end of chapter 4 I contrasted autonomy and authenticity, and we are now in a position to spell out more precisely the ethical aspects of that distinction. Among all moral sentiments, an ethic of autonomy prizes most the courage to stand by one's ethical intuitions even when one is incapable of bringing them in agreement with the expectations of the community. The ethic of authenticity also puts a high value upon this quality, but prizes another kind of courage even more: namely, the courage to stand by one's ethical intuitions even in the face of one's contingent inability to work them out in the language of abstract reflection. From the standpoint of the evolution of ethics, all ethics of authenticity try to respond to the modern tension between morality and self-realization. Usually, such a response consists of introducing a distinction between *peripheral* needs and feelings on one hand and, on the other hand, *central* needs and feelings. The latter receive their privileged status from their being closely linked with a person's sense of identity. The peripheral needs *can* and *should* be modified, either in a positive or in a negative direction, whenever our moral judgment so demands. The feelings bound up with our identity, however, *cannot* be mastered or modified in the same way without generating self-alienation and depersonalization. Thus, according to an ethic of authenticity, they should *not* be put under the jurisdiction of moral judgment in the same direct way as the peripheral needs and feelings. This distinction raises for the ethic of authenticity the challenge of sorting out, within an identity, the needs and feelings which belong to the center from those which are peripheral. This challenge can be met by attributing to the faculty of taste a major role within the process of moral deliberation and by abolishing the distinction, typical of the ethic of autonomy, between abstract principles and their application. Generally, all ethics of authenticity incorporate the hermeneutic insight that the right cannot be determined independently of the situation that requires a right action from us.[1] This does not imply a renunciation of universalism as such, but only of a certain kind of modern universalism. Whereas the ethic of autonomy grounds its universalistic claim on general principles whose validity can be demonstrated through logical reasoning, the ethic of authenticity grounds the universal validity of its pronouncements on the cogent but undemonstrable quality of reflective judgment.[2] For different reasons none of the authors representative of the "tradition of authenticity" has explicitly worked out the relation between authenticity and judgment. Kierkegaard does not address the problem because his concern with authenticity has to do with the existential attitude of the actor who, before entering the world of morality, must decide whether to adopt the moral point of view, rather than with the dynamics of ethical judgment per se. Nietzsche suggests that the judgment of taste as it occurs in the aesthetic realm should replace the illusory universalism and "objectivity" of the Western idea of truth and of moral rightness. However, because he understands aesthetics not as the locus of a special kind of rationality, but as the "antagonist" of rationality, he precludes himself any further insights into the form of rationality implicit in aesthetic judgment. Heidegger, since his ambition is to place his philosophy before the bifurcation of the theoretical and practical paths, rules out the legitimacy of any inquiry into an ethics separate from ontology.[3] Despite references to "Mitsein" and "Fürsorge," no relation with others really matters to "Dasein" in any sense commensurable to the extent that escaping the world of "das Man" and becoming a "Self" matters. Thus the only content of judgment is the extent to which one is becoming oneself. But, again, Heidegger has little to say on the dynamics of that judgment. In *Being and Nothingness* Sartre gives the theme of authenticity an atomistic twist. It seems as though the individual could authentically will *anything* and could, out of his or her will alone, create the *ought* or, actually, a retrospective *ought to have been*. Thus, the project of working out the normativity *sui generis*, universalistic yet undemonstrable and singular, inherent in reflective judgment or in *phronesis*, remains in my opinion a largely unfinished task. Such reconstruction remains, however, a necessary condition for spelling out fully the alternative model of rationality—that is, alternative to the generalizing kind of universalism typical of early-modern thought[4]—presupposed by the tradition of the ethic of authenticity and sometimes brought to surface, within that tradition, under the suggestive names of the "universel singulier" (Sartre) or the "individuelle Gesetz" (Simmel).[5]

The response given by our ethical tradition to the modern tensions of morality is marked by a noticeable imbalance. In fact, the mainstream of Western ethical thought after the Protestant ethic has generally failed to pay adequate attention to the relation of morality to self-realization and has focused more on responding to the other tension of modern morality: the relative lack of motivation for social solidarity. The most common response has taken the form of an attempt to provide foundations for a moral standpoint more general, more abstract and ultimately superior to the concrete morality embedded in social relations already pervaded by strategic orientations. The justification of this superior standpoint was the contribution that ethical reflection could offer, in the eyes of Kant, Fichte or Hegel, in order to offset the hegemony that the strategic orientations of the market and of a secularized polity were gradually gaining throughout society. The ways of pursuing this objective are quite different and sometimes opposite to one another. Kant seeks to ground "pure morality" in an abstract and formal principle (which in turn is part of a practical reason in which all human beings partake) in the hope of removing all reference to historical specificities. Hegel tries a quite different approach. Scorning the self-righteous ineffectuality of a formal morality disjoined from reference to historical reality, Hegel anchored his conception of modern, yet nonstrategic, social relations in the vision of an emancipated community organized in a state "with good laws." Marx took this futurization of the ethical standard as his starting point and investigated the historical and social conditions of its realization. Within the utilitarian tradition the discussion has focused on the exact meaning of the principle of the greatest happiness for the largest number of people. Also in this case it has been taken for granted that the main concern of ethics is the grounding of the sound or rational principles of choice, to be applied whenever self-interest and the interest in justice collide and against which to evaluate the soundness of actual deliberations.

The second tension of modern morality, which concerns the relation of ethical conduct to self-realization, has never been thematized to a comparable extent. However, the presence of this tension can be perceived even in the work of those thinkers who were least interested in questions of self-realization. The case of Kant is one of the most interesting and I would like to discuss it briefly.

Kant does not distinguish between isolated inclinations and inclinations or feelings that are rooted in one's self-identity. Under the same heading of "happiness" (Glückseligkeit) he groups both the satisfaction of occasional desires and the fulfilment of deep-seated character traits. The pursuit of happiness, if elevated to a guiding principle of one's conduct, is the presented by Kant as "the opposite of morality."[6] This is not to say that one should give up happiness in order to achieve moral worthiness, but rather that "as soon as something becomes a matter of duty, no consideration is given to one's happiness any longer."[7] All the examples used by Kant in order to illustrate why the search for happiness results in immoral conduct are formulated at the level of "surface"-conduct, as it were. Somebody appropriates a cash deposit entrusted to him, another fails to keep his promise, a third person bears false witness, and so on. Not a single example can be found, throughout Kant's work, in which the inclinations conflicting with duty are fundamental constituents of the actor's identity. The few passages which indicate some awareness of the problem on Kant's part contain no hint at a solution and let us understand that, *were* Kant to elaborate a solution for the modern tension of morality and self-realization, certainly his solution would not emphasize selffulfilment. Any individual, even the most wicked, argues Kant in the *Groundwork of the Metaphysics of Morals*, when presented with examples of honesty in purpose, of faithfulness to good maxims, of sympathy and kindness, wishes in some way that he too could be a person of that kind. Although the individual might be unable to attain such high standards, due to his desires and impulses, at least he will then wish

> to be free from these inclinations, which are a burden to himself.... From the fulfilment of this wish he can expect no gratification of his sensuous desires and consequently no state which would satisfy any of his actual or even conceivable inclinations;...all he can expect is a greater inner worth of his person.[8]

Disputable in this formulation is the presupposition that feelings and emotions can only be a source of trouble for the moral actor and have somehow to be forced into agreement with one's sense of duty. In this and many other passages we can hear an echo of the 'residual' view of the affects which we encountered in Protestantism—namely, the view that, because there is no special merit in doing one's duty *with* spontaneous inclination and pleasure, feelings, emotions and passions can only get in the way of moral duty.[9] This separation of inner nature and the moral law has given rise to many of the objections moved against Kant's moral philosophy. In reply to Schiller's ideal of a harmonious personality endowed with both grace and dignity and to Schiller's reproach that these two qualities had been split apart in the *Critique of Practical Reason*, Kant granted that "by very reason of the *dignity* of the *idea of duty*" he was "unable to associate *grace* with it." That was because "duty involves absolute necessity, to which grace stands in direct contradiction."[10] Throughout his late work *Religion within the Limits of Reason Alone*, Kant tries to mitigate somehow the rigorist implications of his ethics. He wishes to retain a role for God's forgiveness, because he understands that the stringency of his requirement for moral conduct (to act always and solely out of respect for the categorical imperative) will leave no one unguilty. If nobody can really meet the moral standard then despair and lack of self-confidence will probably ensue and will most likely undermine further the actor's good disposition. Thus Kant wishes to allow for the possibility of atonement and divine forgiveness as God's way to cut down to a human size the requirements of morality and to lighten the burden of guilt which all of us have to carry. This is not to mean that one could exact forgiveness from God through religious rituals, but rather that

> whoever, with a disposition genuinely devoted to duty, does as much as lies in his power to satisfy his obligation (at least in a continual approximation to complete harmony with the law), may hope that what is not in his power will be supplied by the Supreme Wisdom *in some way or other*.[11]

Again, this formulation is quite problematical. In fact, if somebody has truly done "as much as lies in his power" in order to abide by the moral principle, then he does not *need* forgiveness on God's part, even by Kantian standards. On the other hand, if one has not done all that was in one's power, then one does not *deserve* forgiveness and the bestowment of grace upon him constitutes an infringement of the law which is unthinkable as a divine act. Rightly, Kant calls this whole predicament a mystery and, at times, also a contradiction.[12] This contradiction, which Kant did not consider important enough to treat it as another *antinomy of reason*, can be seen as a reflection of the modern tension between morality and self-realization and as evidence for the difficulty of screening out that tension completely even from one of the most consistent ethics of autonomy.

On the whole, Kant's ethic is pervaded by a deep imbalance. On one hand, the *Critique of Practical Reason* constitutes an implicit response to the threat of a potential degradation of social relations to mere strategic relations. At its core lies the distinction between treating others as "ends" (i.e., with full respect of their own will) and treating them as "means" (i.e., instrumentally). In this sense, Kant's ethic consolidates all the most innovative aspects of the Protestant morality—such as (a) the autonomy of moral conscience, and (b) the orientation toward unifying one's action into a life-theme which then grounds one's identity—but at the same time includes a much stronger emphasis on social solidarity. An entire section of the *Metaphysics of Morals* is dedicated by Kant to the duty to love one's neighbor, which is presented as one of the duties "unto others." Love for one's neighbor, which Kant invites us to see not as an "emotional" love but as a disinterested benevolence, is supposed to include (a) charity, (b) gratitude and (c) compassion. Charity is then defined by Kant as helping others to attain happiness, but without any hope to gain anything for oneself therefrom.[13] Another section is dedicated to friendship and its ethical presuppositions, among which Kant stresses especially the nonutilitarian quality of the expectation for mutual help. Friends help each other without any view of future returns. Finally, friendship is presented as involving a mutual disclosure of secret judgments and feelings.[14]

On the other hand, very little attention is paid by Kant to the relation of morality to inner nature. First, the existence of a moral disposition in man is taken for granted. One orients oneself almost naturally to the categorical imperative. On this score, as on many others, Kant took inspiration from Rousseau's own version of an ethic of autonomy, as developed in *The Social Contract* and in *Emile*.[15] Second, acquaintance with the deeper aspects of one's inner nature is seen under an ambivalent light. Insofar as such acquaintance is understood as *knowing* the tendencies of one's personality it is welcomed and encouraged. As Kant says in a rare emphatic passage, "only the descent into the hell of self-knowledge opens the way to sanctity."[16] On the other hand, to the extent that acquaintance with one's emotional world requires an attitude of *acceptance* of our unwanted and despicable inner traits, Kant's ethic, like the Puritan ethic, shows no proclivity towards such acquaintance. The contingencies of one's personality structure, emotional responses and inclinations continue to be seen by Kant as an "internal enemy" of practical reason.[17] Access to moral virtue is conceived as the result of a successful war against the influence of inner nature upon the will.

After Kant, Western ethics has continued to develop mainly along the lines of an ethic of autonomy, while ethical debate has continued to be centered around the best way to ground an ethical standpoint superior to the community's mores or around the alleged impossibility of doing so. Among Kant's critics, Hegel has dwelled to a larger extent on the imbalance mentioned above. His argument against Kant's ethic involves several points, which cannot be here reviewed in detail.[18] Briefly, he accuses Kant of reducing the moral law to little more than a requirement that the will be consistent and tries to show that some bad actions could pass the generalization test while some good ones could be blocked by it.[19] Second, Hegel tries to show that the formal character of the generalization procedure is only a pretense. In fact, the action of appropriating a cash deposit and that of helping a poor man would, if generalized, result in the disappearance respectively of the institution of property and the reality of poverty. In both cases from the test emerges the incompatibility of the maxim underlying the action and the concept (property or poverty) presupposed by the action under examination. Yet in one case we regard the action as right and in the other as wrong. This is possible, argues Hegel, only in so far as we know in advance what is worth preserving and what is not. Therefore the categorical imperative constitutes no standard, but merely reconfirms what we already believe to be good or bad. Consequently, the Kantian way of grounding ethics cannot be regarded as "formal," but on the contrary appears to rest on a hidden and unthematized substantive basis.[20] Third, Hegel accuses Kant's ethic of being unable to generate new maxims of conduct, but to merely pass judgment on existing ones.[21] Fourth, because for Kant moral judgment tests norms and maxims considered in isolation, Hegel criticizes the Kantian ethic for being unable to consider the functional interconnection of norms and institutions within a coherent totality.

Rather than in any of these arguments, however, the gist of Hegel's critique of Kant's moral philosophy consists in the accusation of adopting a one-sided concept of reason. The problem with Kant's philosophy in general, and not just with his ethical theory, is, according to Hegel, that because Kant holds an "abstract" notion of reason, the various aspects either of experience (sense-data and a priori forms of perceptions) or of action (duty and inclinations) never come to a real "mediation" but remain conceptually separate and isolated from one another. To the ineffectual doctrine of duty propounded by Kant, Hegel opposes the anticipation of an ideal state of culture which would make all separate ethical doctrine superfluous. To the abstract "Moralität" of the philosopher he opposes the "Sittlichkeit" of an ideal community yet to come where inner nature and duty will be reconciled and where everyone will spontaneously act in a just way.

One of the most interesting formulations of this theme can be found in the early fragment on "The Spirit of Christianity." Here Hegel directs his criticism against Kant's lack of concern for the relation of morality to identity and, more specifically, against the conception of the person underlying Kant's position. For Kant the highest point of individuation and selfhood coincides with the highest degree of moral worthiness and this, in turn, coincides with those moments when a person's ability to act in accordance with the moral law is at its highest. Just as Rousseau did one generation earlier, the young Hegel also calls into question this vision of morality and the person. For Hegel there exists something even more valuable than respect for the categorical imperative: that is, a life-form in which duty and inclination are reconciled and the tension between morality and self-realization is dissolved. In this form of life, anticipated in the Sermon of the Mountain, people do their duty with pleasure. Thus one cannot speak of duty in the usual sense, but should rather speak of a new unity of feeling and the moral law. The substance of this ethical life, in which emotions and inclinations are no longer the antagonist of reason, is given by love for one's neighbor. Accordingly, the most important moral quality is the person's capacity to love others and to infuse love into his or her acts. Even more important from my own point of view is the fact, stressed over and over by Hegel, that the new moral life he advocates does not simply require us to "support the moral disposition through an appropriate inclination"— which would be a mere 'sincerity'-requirement—but rather requires that the moral disposition of the person be *free of conflict* (eine moralische Gesinnung ohne Kampf), i.e. *authentic* in a psychological sense.[22]

This felicitous way of addressing theoretically both the deficit of solidarity and the surplus of self-repression linked with modernity, however, was but a transient stage in Hegel's intellectual development. Soon it gave way to a new imbalance of emphasis, and again to the detriment of the question of morality in its relation to identity and inner nature. From the Jena period up to his *The Philosophy of Right*, Hegel's ethical views shifted considerably. In a famous aphorism, he suggests that the best answer to a father wondering about the best moral education for his son is: "make him a citizen of a state with good laws."[23] Because no such state yet exists, the aphorism assumes the depositary of true morality to be an ideal community projected into the future. Ethics as such is then deemphasized. It is more important to understand and favor the historical process that will lead us to that future stage, at which the state with good laws will be a reality—a process seen by Hegel as the unfolding of Spirit through human history up to a complete reconciliation of reason and reality, of nature and culture, of society and the self. At the end of human evolution (i.e., at the stage of Absolute Spirit) opacity will no longer haunt social action. No pattern of social action will exist which has been unintentionally created by man. Hegel's view of ethics, however, is not complete without his ideas on the philosophy of history.

In the introduction to his lectures on the philosophy of history, Hegel stresses how progress toward the ideal state and culture depends also on human action and especially on the conduct of the so-called world-historical individuals. These individuals, who often are motivated by the pursuit of their own advantage, are the tools of Reason in that through their actions the World Spirit asserts itself against the contingent configurations of "what is." Individuals such as Caesar, Alexander or Napoleon

> have no consciousness of the Idea as such. They are practical and political men. But at the same time they are thinkers with insight into what is needed and timely. They see the very truth of their age and their worlds, the next genus, so to speak, which is already formed in the womb of time. It is theirs to know this new universal, the necessary next stage of their world, to make it their own aim and put all their energy into it.[24]

In their actions they "trample down many an innocent flower," but it would be futile to judge them according to the standard of "private" morality. For the world-historical individuals "stand outside of morality" and "the litany of the private virtues of modesty, humility, love and charity must not be raised against them."[25] As Hegel puts it, "the history of the world moves on a higher level than that proper to morality" and "the demands and accomplishments of the absolute and final aim of Spirit...lie above the obligations, responsibilities and liabilities which are incumbent on the individuals in regard to their morality."[26]

In the ethical position of the late Hegel the old repressive attitude toward the emotional part of the self—so sharply criticized by the young Hegel in his polemic against Kant—is reintroduced with full force. The great man who grows to a world-historical role is able to do so because, different from the petty man or the victim of history, he is willing to sacrifice his private happiness to greatness. There is little merit for Hegel in a life devoted to happiness and the realization of one's identity in the *private* sphere. Only the individual who realizes his identity in the accomplishment of a task of universal significance has lived a worthy life. Private virtue is degraded to the morality of "schoolmasters" or "valets de chambre" and is seen as a disguise for envy as well as a rationalization of one's inability to attain greatness—a theme later developed by Nietzsche in *The Genealogy of Morals*. Ironically, the ethic implicit in the position of the late Hegel restores the same split between Reason and inner nature which the young Hegel had so effectively criticized in Kant. The world-historical individual achieves greatness by renouncing those aspects of his identity which, if cultivated, would confine his life to a merely private significance, and those who fail, the victims of history, do so mostly because they indulge in the search for a personal and private happiness. Not only is the split between inner nature and the rational part of man reintroduced, but this split, which in Kant stemmed from the intention to preserve the unconditional quality of the moral law, in Hegel becomes enmeshed with a potentially cynical perspective. One of the conclusions consistent with Hegel's philosophy of history is that it is important not so much to educate one's character in such a way that one will be brought by one's inclinations to fulfil the duties of morality, as to attain that greatness, cost what may, which will then put one beyond the reach of the common moral standards.

Two considerations come to mind when one reflects on the significance of Hegel's ethical position not so much for the history of philosophy but for the evolution of the modern form of moral discourse. From the standpoint of the rationalization of Western ethical thought, Hegel's vision of morality represents an ambiguous turning point. The positive side of this ambiguity is constituted by Hegel's strong emphasis on the *functional interconnection* of social action and on the *objective consequences* of conduct. Hegel reverses the Protestant and the Kantian insistence on *intentions* as the basis for evaluating conduct. For him the objective consequences of an action, especially its potential contribution to progress towards the "state with good laws," count more than the subjective intention of the actor who performed the action. In a sense, Hegel's view entails a further enlargement of the object of moral judgment. What is to be morally judged is the person's life-conduct considered not only under the aspect of its underlying intention (as in Calvin's and Kant's ethics), but also under the aspect of its objective consequences and, more specifically, of its potential contribution to historical progress. This innovative aspect of Hegel's conception of ethics, however, is counterbalanced by his inability to provide a satisfactory response to the two modern tensions which he originally set out to resolve. On the one hand, his position provides less ground for social solidarity than Kant's. In fact, Hegel's ethic does not prohibit but actually justifies treating others as means to a superior design to which they have given no consent. On the other hand, the late Hegel's position fails to accomplish that reconciliation of the tension between morality and inner nature which constituted one of the aims of the young Hegel. In fact, Hegel's view of history merely replaces the old command to sacrifice happiness to duty with a new exhortation to sacrifice happiness to *greatness*.

On the whole, Hegel's influence has contributed to the consolidation of the ethic of autonomy in the mainstream of Western moral thought. More specifically, it has contributed to drive the themes of identity and self-realization out of systematic ethical reflection. This effect is best illustrated by the devaluation of ethics and the distrust for 'personal' ways to self-realization typical of the Marxist tradition.

In the light of these cursory remarks we can better understand the significance of Rousseau's implicit ethic of authenticity. First, Rousseau's contribution to the rationalization of Western ethic after the rise of Calvinism and to the shaping of the contemporary moral climate consists in his providing a *balanced* response to the tensions generated by the hegemony of Puritanism. In the "Second Discourse," Rousseau exposed the potential for the reification of social relations inherent in possessive individualism. In his critique of the *unsociable sociability* promoted by Puritanism Rousseau is in the company of Kant, Hegel and Marx. Yet implicit in *The New Heloise* we find a post-conventional ethic of authenticity which posits self-cohesion as a domain where ethical prescriptions should have no direct jurisdiction. This conception of ethics can be taken as a response to the repressive rigidity of the Puritan morality of autonomy in that it contains the distinction between peripheral and central needs of an identity and the idea that the latter should *not* be put under the direct jurisdiction of moral principles in the same way as the rest of our desires or inclinations. No ethical principle can prescribe us to become another person. As we have seen, the introduction of this distinction raises the problem of identifying the needs which belong to the center of an identity, but no answer to this question can be found in Rousseau.

Second, implicit in Rousseau's social and ethical thought is a critique of the "productivist" conceptions of self-realization which arose with early modernity and later became predominant. For Puritanism the good life is a life spent in shaping the external world through work and internal nature through the will. Only the activity of producing and giving shape to something can confer dignity upon one's existence and cohesion to one's identity. For Hegel work and selfdiscipline must be complemented by a third, and more important, ingredient of a worthy life, i.e. the attempt to bind one's individual existence with the universal development of Spirit. Only those who renounce private gratification or happiness and gain access to a world-historical role have lived a truly worthy life. Marx gave this conception a new turn without changing it substantially. A worthy life is for him a life spent in the attempt to free society from alienated relations of production. A different emphasis can be found in Rousseau. For him the good life does not entail the production of any object, even in the metaphorical sense of the production of new social relations. For even though our personal identity can be formed only in the context of an exchange with the external world, this exchange need not be understood in terms of production or transformation, but may consist of inscribing the underlying pattern of the self into a set of personal relationships. Today, when the Hegelian emphasis on the priority of constructing the "state with good laws" over seeking a private fulfilment of the self has lost much of its suggestiveness, Rousseau's radical critique of the early-modern myth of "homo faber" cannot but appear more timely.

Finally, Rousseau can be credited for being the first to have attempted to reconcile authenticity in a psychological sense with a modern morality of principle. He has initiated a way of thinking about man, modernity and morality which revolves around the notion of being oneself or of authenticity and which, through the work of Schiller, the young Hegel, Kierkegaard, Nietzsche and Heidegger, extends to our contemporary culture. These authors, who do not understand their work as the development of a unique core of thought and therefore do not form a tradition in the usual sense of the term, all share a strong emphasis on authenticity. Despite their divergences, they share three ideas. First, they presuppose a notion of the human being according to which the *capacity for being oneself* is the fundamental feature of the person. This notion is implicit in Rousseau's moral psychology, in Kierkegaard's reflections on aesthetic and ethical life, in Nietzsche's characterization of Zarathustra and in Heidegger's definition of *Dasein*. Second, these authors criticize Western modernity from the standpoint of authenticity. Namely, they accuse the spirit of differentiation dominant throughout early modernity of having undermined the individual's capacity to become him- or herself. This accusation is formulated in terms of a critique of "social reproduction through competition" by Rousseau, in terms of a study of the existential presuppositions of ethical conduct by Kierkegaard, in terms of a critique of the cultural repression of Dionysian forces by Nietzsche, and in terms of a critique of the neglect of the question of Being on the part of Western metaphysics by Heidegger. Finally, all these authors bring back to center-stage the relation of morality to selfrealization. This is done only indirectly by Rousseau in *The New Heloise*, it is done by Kierkegaard through his insistence on the theme of self-choice and through his analysis of the "sickness unto death," by Nietzsche through his critique of the naive universalism of Western ethics in the *Genealogy of Morals*, and by Heidegger through his distinction of the "They" and "Authentic There-Being."

At closer inspection, to be sure, underneath this common ground impressive differences can be found among Kierkegaard, Nietzsche and Heidegger. In light of these differences the use of term "tradition of authenticity" may appear almost metaphorical and the understanding of the work of these authors as a contribution to the process of *ethical* rationalization may seem even more problematical. In fact, while Kierkegaard's argument in *Either/Or* presupposes the meaningfulness of the moral law and the moral life, Nietzsche's main point in the *Genealogy of Morals* is to call that presupposition into question. Furthermore, Heidegger's understanding of his own inquiry as topographically located *before* the bifurcation of theoretical and practical philosophy—a bifurcation bound up with a deeply distorted understanding of the nature of Being—leads him time and again to declare ethics altogether unimportant as a terrain of philosophical debate. Nevertheless, the undeniable existence of these different attitudes toward the Western ethical tradition—Kierkegaard's inquiring about the existential, as opposed to a merely conceptual, viability of the moral point of view, Nietzsche's denouncing the moral point of view as the main manifestation, influenced by Christianity, of a distorted will to power, and Heidegger's dismissing it as largely inconsequential and irrelevant—should not blind one to the fact that these three philosophers all try to justify their stances, in one vocabulary or another, by reference to the idea of "being oneself," "choosing oneself," or "becoming who one is." Furthermore, these authors in various ways denounce the *generalizing* universalism of modernity and point to a kind of individualizing, singular and exemplary universalism based ultimately on the same idea of self-congruity which underlies our appreciation of the aesthetically wellformed work of art. Finally, insofar as their arguments have an ethical relevance, these authors have more to say about the good than about the right and tend to understand the good as authenticity. Kierkegaard, for example, clearly brings the concept of authenticity at the center of his ethical view, when he writes that the object of choice is "the absolute," understood as "myself in my eternal validity." "Anything else but myself," argues Kierkegaard, "I never can choose as the absolute, for if I choose something else, I choose it as a finite thing and so do not choose it absolutely."[27] Against the standard version of the ethic of autonomy, in a vein reminiscent of Schiller's point about grace and dignity, writes Kierkegaard,

> In opposition to an aesthetical view which would enjoy life, one often hears of another view which finds the significance of life in living for the fulfilment of its duties. With this one intends to indicate an ethical life view. However the expression is very imperfect, and one might almost believe that it was invented in order to bring the ethical into disrepute.... The fault is that the individual is placed in an outward relation to duty. The ethical is defined as duty, and duty in turn is defined as a congeries of particular propositions, but the individual and duty stand outside of one another.[28]

On the other hand Nietzsche's attack on morality as the product of the "herd instinct" and as the "bad-faith" attempt, on the part of the weak, to self-enthrone themselves as the "good ones" in order to prevent the strong-willed from asserting themselves,[29] presupposes the notion of a superior morality—namely, a morality of excellence whose supreme virtue is courage in asserting one's will to power. This morality even has a cognitivistic corollary in the philosopher's task of "solving the problem of value" by determining "the true hierarchy of value."[30] The ethical valence of Nietzsche's "immoralism" could be summed up in his point that Western ethics, and especially modern ethics, by putting the notion of justice at center-stage, has forfeited the individual's chance to attain the good life, which Nietzsche construes as the pursuit of an unlimited self-realization.

Finally, Heidegger's claim that his analysis of the structure of human existence, his *Daseinsanalyse*, has no ethical import in that it is located at the level of a "fundamental ontology," carries weight only insofar as we understand the terms 'ethics' and 'ethical' along the lines of an ethic primarily centered on the notion of justice and on the question "What is the relation between acting justly and pursuing one's interest?". Only from the standpoint of the competing tradition of autonomy and its search for general ethical principles can one take seriously Heidegger's claim that his conception of *Dasein* has no ethical import. In a less reductive view of ethics it seems difficult to deny that the very idea of *Dasein*'s transcending the world of "das Man" and becoming a self, or Heidegger's analysis of the authentic "Being unto death"[31] as the way of life more appropriate for a being whose distinctive characteristic is that "Being is an issue for it," indeed continue under modern premises the ancient discourse of the good life, or are arguments concerning the good.

The ramifications of the idea of authenticity implicit in these authors and their implications for the rationalization of the modern ethos, however, cannot be investigated in the context of the present study. They call for an entire new inquiry.

NOTES

NOTES TO INTRODUCTION

1. For a discussion of the meaning of the term modernity, see Habermas 1985: 9–21.

NOTES TO CHAPTER 1

1. Sennett 1978: 259. For very similar views, see also Lasch 1980: 188, 195, and Riesman 1964: 155.

2. Weber 1905: 13.

3. See Riesman 1980: 21, Bell 1976: 7 and Rieff 1973: 224.

4. See Bell 1976: 33–34.

5. Bell 1976: 49–50. See also Bell 1980: 275–302.

6. Bell 1976: 50.

7. Bell 1976: 19.

8. Bell 1976: 21.

9. See Bell 1976: 41 and 149. About Bell's explanation for the diffusion of the adversary culture it must be observed, however, that this diffusion pre-

supposes the decline of the Protestant ethic in two ways—i.e. as a necessary condition for the elite's modernistic outlook to spread into the larger society, but also as a necessary condition for the elite to be attracted to aesthetic modernism in the first place. In *The Winding Passage* Bell for the first time introduces a new element in his explanation. This new element is the diffusion of a therapeutic outlook linked with the proliferation of (often misinterpreted) Freudian ideas. However, this new theme is not developed to any extent comparable with Bell's account of aesthetic modernism. See Bell 1980: 288.

10. Bell 1976: 30. In his essay "The Return of the Sacred?", Bell offers his speculations on the form that a religious revival could possibly take in the West. See Bell 1980: 348–51.

11. See Riesman 1964. At the time when it first appeared, Riesman's study stirred up a lively debate on the "changing American character." Many voices were raised against his thesis and in defense of a "continuity"-thesis or of a "nothing new under the sun"-position. See Parsons and White 1964, Kluckhohn 1958 and Lipset 1961.

12. Riesman 1964: 21.

13. Riesman 1964: 47–48.

14. Riesman 1964: 49.

15. For instance, see Lasch 1980: 159–68 and Strzyz 1981: 109–15.

16. Riesman 1964: 60–65.

17. See Riesman 1963: 109–10.

18. See Riesman 1980: 21.

19. Rieff 1961: 391. For a characterization of "political man," "economic man" and "psychological man" as the personality types dominant respectively in the premodern, the early modern and the contemporary world, see Rieff 1961: 391–92.

20. Rieff 1973: 217. On the impact of the therapeutic mentality upon morality see Rieff 1975: 150–52.

21. Rieff 1973: 205.

22. Rieff 1973: 19–24.

23. Rieff 1973: 24.

24. On the erosion of public life, see Sennett 1978: 3–4. On the ideology of intimacy, see Sennett 1978: 259. For similar remarks on intimacy, see Lasch 1980: 188, 195 and Riesman 1964: 155.

25. On the notion of "soft despotism," see Tocqueville 1969: 691–93.

26. Sennett 1978: 264.

27. Sennett 1978: 4.

28. See Sennett 1978: 177–83.

29. Sennett 1978: 21.

30. For a criticism of Sennett along similar lines, see Lasch 1980: 27–30. Sennett's inability to envision any remedy other than a sheer return to the forms of classical modernity can be seen most clearly in his discussion of the two modalities of authority, namely "authority without love" and the "authority of false love," Sennett 1980: 50–121.

31. Sennett 1978: 5.

32. Lasch 1980: 25.

33. Lasch 1980: 230.

34. Lasch 1980: 13.

35. See Kohut 1971, 1977 and Kernberg 1975.

36. Lasch 1980: 27.

37. Lasch 1980: 27.

38. See Lasch 1984. On social causes see Lasch 1980: 231.

39. A similar position can be found also in the work of other theorists concerned with modernity. For example, see Berger, Berger and Kellner 1973, Berger 1979, Nisbet 1969, Mumford 1970, Gehlen 1956, Gehlen 1957.

40. See Feyerabend 1975, Derrida 1976, 1978, 1981 and 1982, Lyotard 1979, Rorty 1980 and 1989, Foucault 1975 and 1984, Lacan 1977 and 1978, Deleuze and Guattari 1977.

41. For example, see Sennett 1978: 3–4.

42. For a critique of neoconservatism along these lines see Habermas 1981b and 1983a. See also Swanson 1980.

43. Bellah 1970: 246. See also Bellah 1985 and Smelser 1980.

44. Walzer maintains that while on one hand criteria for justice cannot be specified independently of an account of the society where they are supposed to work, on the other hand for every existing society arrangements exist that could be recognized as arrangements of that society and be just. Basically, to be unjust for a society means that what takes place in one distributive sphere violates conceptions that exist in some other part of the collective representation of the goods in question. The predicate 'just', in other words, is understood as "just in its own terms." See Walzer 1983, ch. 13. See also "Three Paths in Moral Philosophy," in Walzer 1987. According to Dworkin, the rightness of a sentence in a controversial legal case does not rest on its susceptibility to be derived from a procedure for legal decision-making,

for the axiomatic unspecifiability of such a procedure is precisely what makes the role of the judge necessary, but rests on its being, among all the possible sentences, the one which "makes the most" of the entire legal, jurisprudential as well as historical tradition of the country. See Dworkin 1986, ch. 7. See also Dworkin 1985, ch. 6.

45. In *After Virtue* the point was merely touched upon in passing; see MacIntyre 1981: 207. For the notion of the superiority of an ethical tradition defined as the capacity of a tradition to undergo progress, where progress is understood as the capacity to progressively and constructively respond to challenges, see MacIntyre 1988: 361–62. See also MacIntyre 1990.

NOTES TO CHAPTER 2

1. Kant 1980: 282.

2. Among the supporters of the 'realist' interpretation, see Lovejoy 1948, Masters 1968, Strauss 1953 and Plattner 1979. The rationalist position is represented by Burgelin 1952, Durkheim 1965, Charvet 1974, Launay 1971, Levi-Strauss 1973 and Cassirer 1954. Cassirer, however, insists on the confusion that Rousseau must have had on the matter. Whereas in the "Second Discourse," according to Cassirer, it is clear that Rousseau neither could nor wanted to describe a historically demonstrable original state of mankind (Cassirer 1954: 50), in the "Dialogues" Rousseau describes himself as "the first truthful 'historian of human nature'" (Cassirer 1963: 24). This discrepancy, however, does not show that the confusion existed at the time when the "Discourse" was written. Derathé 1950 and Vaughan 1960 portray a Rousseau who "does not know what he wants" even in the context of the "Discourse." Finally, a very perceptive interpreter of Rousseau such as Starobinski also oscillates on the issue. In his essay "La transparence et l'obstacle" (Starobinski 1971: 11–316) he argues that Rousseau starts out with treating the state of nature as a methodological fiction, only to be carried away, after a few paragraphs, into a pseudohistorical account. In the essay "Le Discours sur l'origine et les fondements de l'inégalité" (Starobinski 1971: 330–55) the ambiguity is resolved in favor of a rationalist interpretation.

3. Rousseau 1755: 177.

4. See Marx 1957: 83.

5. Rousseau 1755: 171.

6. Rousseau 1755: 202.

7. See Rousseau 1755: 187.

8. Rousseau 1755: 186

9. See Charvet 1974: 9.

10. See Hobbes 1972: 186. On the state of nature, see chapter XIII of *Leviathan*: Hobbes 1972: 183–88.

11. Kant makes a similar point when he underscores that envy, in gratitude, spitefulness and "open animosity against all whom we look upon as
not belonging to us" are all "vices of culture" (Kant 1960: 22). See also Kant's
"Conjectural Beginning of Human History," in Kant 1963: 53–68, especially
p. 60.

12. Rousseau 1755: 256.

13. See Charvet 1974: 16. 14. Charvet 1974: 17.

15. Charvet believes this to be a serious problem for Rousseau, in that
Rousseau would also be under pressure to find something in human nature
which can serve as the ground for social living. This role should be played by
the notion of 'human', as opposed to generic or animal, pity (Charvet 1974:
19). This interpretation is misleading, because Rousseau's overarching goal is
rather to explain the rise of society *without* resorting to man's propensity
toward association. From *this* point of view it makes much more sense to
keep human pity only degrees apart from that which can be shared by animals too.

16. Rousseau 1755: 218.

17. See Charvet 1974: 30–31.

18. Charvet thinks that it would be inconsistent for Rousseau to allow
for the existence of social bonds in which to orient one's actions to the expectations of other does not result in the rise of competitive feelings. Thus the
Rousseauian idea of a liberated or just society would be inherently contradictory (see Charvet 1974: 32–33).

19. See Rousseau 1755: 220. Actually, Rousseau considered the patriar
chal stage of society happier or more desirable than the state of na ture. On
this point, see Lovejoy 1948: 28 and Casotti 1929: 84.

20. Starobinski has pointed out that the central motif within Rousseau's
thought is constituted by the realization that "being and appearance are two
things" and that in social life necessarily "a 'veil' disguises the true feelings."
To the realm of the veil Rousseau opposes a "realm of transparency," in
which "men manifest themselves and are seen as they really are." See
Starobinski 1971: 15.

21. Cassirer 1954: 75.

22. Philopolis, Letter to Rousseau of 28 August, 1755, in the Pléiade Edition of Rousseau's works, vol. 3, p. 230.

23. "Reply to Philopolis," in the Pléiade Edition of Rousseau's works,
vol. 3, p. 232.

24. See Vaughan 1915: I, 223.

25. Rousseau 1755: 212–13.

26. Rousseau 1755: 213–14.

27. Rousseau 1755: 214.

28. Rousseau 1755: 220.

29. See Rousseau 1755: 220–23.

30. See Rousseau 1755: 223.

31. See Rousseau 1755: 221.

32. See Durkheim 1933: 277.

33. See Rousseau 1755: 222. It is interesting to note the difference with Condorcet's explanation for the rise of the division of labor. Condorcet centers his explanation on the surplus product *already* possessed by some individuals. This surplus, presumably accumulated on the basis of natural inequality and luck, for the first time allows somebody to buy someone else's labor. See Condorcet 1971: 79.

34. Lovejoy suggests that from the account of the transition to the agricultural society one can draw the assumption of a radically evil element in human nature—an assumption which contrasts with the more conventional and eighteenth-century image of human nature of the beginning of the "Discourse" and represents one of the most original ideas in Rousseau's essay. See Lovejoy 1948: 32.

35. Rousseau 1755: 224.

36. On the effects of social complexity on the quality of individual identity Rousseau anticipates some of the ideas later developed by Simmel. For example, both point out that the availability of a larger num ber of roles paradoxically results not in a more solid but in a more fragmented quality of the individual identity. See Simmel 1950: 58–59.

37. See Rousseau 1761: II, 14 (the Roman figure refers to the part of the book and the Arabic one to the number of the letter).

38. Rousseau's argument on the erosion of subjectivity in modern society takes us beyond the "Second Discourse," into the portrait of Paris that he draws in *The New Heloise*. Here, through the eyes of Julie's lover, Rousseau describes his impressions of Parisian life. See Rousseau 1761: II book, letters 14, 16, 17, and 21. For a direct statement of the same impressions, see Rousseau 1770: book 12. Berman points out that whereas criticisms of modern society in terms of insincerity had long been the stock-in-trade of many moralists, Rousseau's critique of modern social life in terms of inauthenticity represents an original contribution. Berman, however, presents the two emphases as sequentially ordered in the development of Rousseau's thought, whereas no such order can really be found. See Berman 1972: 136–44.

39. See Marx 1967: 274–77; Weber 1958: 181–82 and Durkheim 1951: 254–58.

NOTES TO CHAPTER 3

1. Some Marxist interpreters of Rousseau have insisted on this point. See Della Volpe 1974 and Colletti 1972.

2. Rousseau 1755: 257–58.

3. Della Volpe 1974: 40–41.

4. Colletti 1972: 260.

5. From this standpoint it is hard to agree with Wolin when he suggests that both in Durkheim's and in Rousseau's conception of the just society no tension would exist between the self and society. See Wolin 1960: 372.

6. In the *Parisian Manuscripts* some remarks can be found on the reification of human relations due to the effects of power and prestige as "media" for the coordination of social action, but in the passage on "commodity fetishism" of the first book of *Capital* reification is again understood as the result of purely economic processes. See Marx 1967: 301–03.

7. See Crocker 1965, 1967 and 1968; Chapman 1956; Vaughan 1915: 48; and Talmon 1970: 41ff.

8. Rousseau 1762a: 18. The paradoxical quality of the contract envisaged by Rousseau is discussed by L. Althusser. The social contract brings together two parties, one of which (the individual) exists both prior to and externally to the contract, whereas the other (the community) is rather the product of the contract itself. See Althusser 1972: 129.

9. Rousseau 1762a: 43.

10. See Rousseau 1762a: 33.

11. Crocker 1967: xvii.

12. Rousseau's intent is well captured in Durkheim 1965 and Cobban 1934: 88–95.

13. See Rousseau 1762a: 33.

14. See Rousseau 1762a: 35. See also Levine 1976 and Steinberg 1978. For Levine, Rousseau's formulation of this requirement does not suffice to block trivial attempts to contravene it. See Levine 1976: 48.

15. See Rousseau 1762a: 33.

16. See Rousseau 1762a: 55.

17. On Rousseau's thought about social classes see Fetscher 1968: 214–28 and Manfredi 1978: 15–21. On the connection between the totalitarian overtones of some paragraphs of *The Social Contract* and Rousseau's intent to overcome the existence and influence of social class, see Althusser 1972: 155.

18. See Rousseau 1762a: 30. This passage is overlooked by Hegel when he criticizes Rousseau, in the *Lectures on the History of Philosophy*, for absolutizing the particularism of the individual. See Hegel 1971: XX, 307.

19. See Derathé 1950: 245–46.

20. This point is also stressed by Levine. See Levine 1976: 74–75.

21. Lukes 1973: 283.

22. On this point see also Merquior 1980: 51.

23. In the light of these considerations, again, Wolin's contention that in Durkheim's work we can find "the purest restatement of Rousseau" appears disputable. See Wolin 1960: 372.

24. Habermas 1962. For a similar interpretation of Rousseau's views on public opinion, see Shklar 1969: 75–103.

25. See Rousseau 1762a: 41.

26. Rousseau 1762a: 45.

27. See Crocker 1967: xxi.

28. See Rousseau 1762a: 134.

29. See Rousseau 1762a: 146.

30. See Berlin 1958.

31. Berlin 1958: 144.

32. See Fetscher 1968: 237–62. Fetscher must be credited, however, for his otherwise insightful reconstruction of Rousseau's economic views.

33. On Rousseau's notion of freedom as autonomy and for an interesting parallel with Hegel's *Philosophy of Right*, see Bobbio 1975: 99–101.

34. Berlin 1958: 150.

35. For an excellent reconstruction of the liberal notion of the self, see the chapter on "Liberal Psychology" in R. Unger's *Knowledge and Politics*. Unger 1975: 29–62.

36. Berlin 1958: 150.

37. See the chapter on "Legitimation Problems in the Modern State," and especially pp. 184–86, in Habermas 1979, and Habermas 1975: 97–101.

38. See Hegel 1971: VII, para. 124.

39. See Aristotle 1962: books 7 and 8.

40. It is seems questionable to argue that because Rousseau abandons the idea of specifying *a priori* the proper objectives of civil society he has

thereby abandoned all interest in the foundation of political right. See Masters 1968: 422.

41. See Levine 1976: 198. On the evolution of Rousseau's political theory after *The Social Contract*, see Namer 1979: 183–204.

NOTES TO CHAPTER 4

1. For a complete characterization of the principles of "negative education," see Rousseau's letter to Monsignor De Beaumont, Rousseau 1762c.

2. Rousseau 1762b: 5.

3. See Books 1 and 2 of Locke 1965; Locke 1947; and Rousseau 1755: 187.

4. On the relation between Rousseau's, Locke's and Condillac's views on psychology and on the theory of knowledge, see Jimack 1960. On the same theme, but with a stronger emphasis on the anthropological aspects of Rousseau's thought, see Rang 1959. On the sociology of knowledge implicit in Rousseau, see Namer 1978.

5. Rousseau 1762b: 9.

6. For Kant "children ought to be educated, not for the present, but for a possibly improved condition of man in the future; that is, in a manner which is adapted to the *idea of humanity* and the whole destiny of man," Kant 1966: 14.

7. Durkheim 1919: 157. Durkheim's interpretation of the pedagogic aspects of Rousseau's work contains little more than a projection of his own themes and emphases. On the goals of moral education, see Durkheim 1956 and 1961.

8. See parr. 64, 65 and 66 in Locke 1947. See also Burgelin 1952: 485.

9. The similarity between Rousseau's views and the theories of Piaget, Kohlberg and Erikson goes beyond the common emphasis on the discontinuous, irreversible, and crisis-ridden quality of cognitive and moral development. For all these authors development goes in the direction of an expanded capacity for abstract and reflexive reasoning, for consensual forms of interaction and for autonomy. See Piaget 1952a, 1952b, 1954, 1965, Piaget/Inhelder 1956, Inhelder/Piaget 1958, 1964; Kohlberg 1964, 1966, 1969, 1971, 1973; Erikson 1959 and 1963.

10. Rousseau 1762b: 33.

11. The notion of maturity as the ability to strike a balance between desires and abilities is a Stoic theme. See Bretonneau 1977 and Pire 1953.

12. The "raison sensitive" is a rudimentary predecessor of the understanding. Its development represents the equivalent of the stage of "concrete thinking" in Piaget's schema of the development of intelligence. On the difference between the "raison sensitive" and understanding, see Rousseau 1762b: 122.

13. See Rousseau 1762b: 71–72.

14. Rousseau 1762b: 72.

15. Rousseau 1762b: 49.

16. Kant 1966: 54.

17. See Rousseau 1762b: 84–85.

18. See Starobinski 1971: 257. See also Charvet 1974: 56–64.

19. See Rousseau 1762b: 129.

20. See Rousseau 1762b: 130.

21. See Rousseau 1762b: 140. For an elaborate example on "the lesson of things," see Rousseau 1762b: 143–44.

22. See Rousseau 1762b: 169–70.

23. Whereas in the "Second Discourse" pity was considered an innate instinct by Rousseau, now it is said to derive from self-love. See Rousseau 1762b: 196.

24. See Rousseau 1762b: 262–63.

25. See Derathé 1948: 94–97 and Rousseau 1762b: 196.

26. Quoted in Derathé 1948: 115.

27. Kant is much more pragmatic on this score. Whereas Rousseau would have the child only observe manipulation, Kant insists that a modicum of manipulativeness and cynicism must be taught as well. See Kant 1966: 95–6.

28. Rousseau 1762b: 328.

29. Several passages in *Emile* support this interpretation. For example, see Rousseau 1762b: 7 and 130.

30. Mead 1972: 375.

31. See Rousseau 1762b: 246.

32. See Rousseau 1762b: 7.

33. I refer here to the sense in which Freud uses the term 'ego' in Freud 1923. At other times the distinction between ego and self is very tenuous in Freud (for example, see Freud 1914 and 1930). On Freud's concept of the self, see Hartmann 1964. For a discussion on the distinction between self and ego, see Schafer 1976: 102–20.

34. See Szasz 1974: 28 and 102–03; Menninger 1958: 93–98.

35. Trilling 1971: 10–11.

36. On the distinction between sincerity (good faith) and authenticity, see also Sartre 1966: 112–16 and 116 fn.

37. Trilling 1971: 94.

38. See Sartre's discussion of the waiter character, Sartre 1966: 101–03. For a similar argument, centered on the notion of honor rather than authenticity, see J. Marx 1980: 188.

39. See Hochschild 1979: 561 and Hochschild 1983.

40. See Cassirer 1963; Levine 1976; Durkheim 1919 and 1960.

41. See Marianne Weber 1950: 418–19. The translation follows Mitzman 1969: 281.

42. For similar and influential formulations of the nature of morality, see Ortega y Gasset 1972: ch. 7, and Dewey 1922.

43. See *Contemporary Psychoanalysis*, vol.18, 3, 1982, p. 309.

44. For example, see Sennett 1978: 337ff.

45. On this aspect of intimacy, see Simmel 1950: 324. On how this requirement of unconditional acceptance affects the patterns of conflict in intimate relationships, see Simmel 1955: 43–48.

46. On the notion of a gift economy, see Mauss 1967.

NOTES TO CHAPTER 5

1. See Crocker 1963: 152 and Crocker 1971.

2. Two notable exceptions are Berman 1972 and Shklar 1969. See also De Jouvenel 1962: 96 fn.

3. Saint-Preux incorporates some of the character traits most valued by Rousseau. On the relation between the novel and Rousseau's life, see Osmont 1953 and Mornet 1928.

4. On Claire, see Shklar 1969: 232.

5. Rousseau 1761: I, 14. See above, chapter 2, footnote 37.

6. Grimsley 1969: 134.

7. Rousseau 1761: II, 3.

8. Rousseau 1761: II, 3.

9. Rousseau 1761: III, 18.

10. On Julie's conversion, see Mauzi 1959.

11. Rousseau 1761: III, 20.

12. Rousseau 1761: 262.

13. Rousseau 1761: IV, 10.

14. Rousseau 1761: IV, 10.

15. Rousseau 1761: IV, 10.

16. Rousseau 1761: IV, 10.

17. Rousseau 1761: V, 2.

18. On Wolmar's manipulativeness, see Crocker 1963: 126–35.

19. See Rousseau 1761: IV, 12.

20. See Rousseau 1761: IV, 13.

21. Rousseau 1761: VI, 8.

22. See Rousseau 1761: VI, 12.

23. On this point, see also Crocker 1963.

24. See Babbitt 1919. On Julie as a beautiful soul see Mauzi 1959, Hall 1962 and Ellis 1949.

25. Duplicity and hypocrisy are two traits of Julie's character on which also L. Crocker has insisted. See Crocker 1963 and Crocker 1971: 52–98. For the typical positive portrait of Julie, see Ellis 1949.

26. See Rousseau 1761: II, 6.

27. See Rousseau 1761; VI, 12.

28. The case of More is suggested by Kant as an example of purity of the moral will, see Kant 1983: 184.

29. On the inner logic of the judgement of taste, and on the affinity of taste with the Aristotelian virtue of *phronesis,* see Gadamer 1975: 33–9, and 278–89. See also Kant 1951: parr. 32 and 33, and Aristotle 1976: Book VI.

30. On this point, see MacIntyre 1984 and Waldron 1989.

31. See Swidler 1980 and Turner 1976.

NOTES TO CHAPTER 6

1. See Wittgenstein 1931: 241.

2. On the relevance of Schiller's view of the self for understanding the conflicts and tensions of contemporary culture, see Taylor 1989: 497–99.

3. See Schiller 1971: 101.

4. See Schiller 1971: 107.

5. See Weber 1978: 399–541.

6. Weber 1958: 13.

7. On Weber's oscillation between a broader and a more reductive concept of rationalization, see Habermas 1981: I, 345.

8. See Schluchter 1981: 39–48.

9. See Kohlberg 1981: I, 17–19.

10. See Kohlberg 1981: I, 19.

11. This term is not given by Weber the same meaning as here. By this term Weber refers both to the ethics of conviction (such as the Puritan ethic) and to the conventional ethics of concrete norms (such as the Ten Commandments). Following Schluchter, I have separated the two and called only the latter a "religious ethic of norms."

12. See Weber 1978: 399–439.

13. Weber 1978: 438.

14. Weber 1978: 533.

15. Weber 1978: 534.

16. See Weber 1975: 323–59.

17. Weber 1975: 329.

18. See Weber 1975: 333.

19. According to Schluchter, this constituted the main contribution of Puritanism to the rise of modern society. See Schluchter 1981: 171–72. For a different view, see Habermas 1981a: I, 311.

20. Weber 1975: 336.

21. See Weber 1975: 341.

22. Weber 1975: 342.

23. Weber 1975: 342.

24. See Weber 1975: 343–50.

25. For a characterization of the transition to a modern morality of principle in these terms, see Habermas 1983b: 187–95.

26. See Weber 1958: 104–06 and Tawney 1980: 229–51.

27. See Weber 1958: 272–74.

28. See Weber 1958: 275.

NOTES TO CHAPTER 7

1. See Gadamer 1975: 283.

2. On the inner logic of reflective judgment, and especially of the judgment of taste, see Gadamer's reconstruction of Kant, Gadamer 1975: 33–39.

3. See Heidegger 1946: 349–60. See also his remarks on the Kantian ethic and the notion of moral law, Heidegger 1973: 251–52.

4. On this point see also Walzer 1990.

5. See Sartre 1966 and Simmel 1987.

6. See Kant 1983: Book I, ch. 1, par. 8.

7. See Kant 1983: 114.

8. See Kant 1964: 122.

9. For a similar criticism, see Schiller 1971: 105.

10. See Kant 1960: 19.

11. See Kant 1960: 159.

12. See Kant 1960: 108.

13. See Kant 1966a: parr. 25, 28, 30.

14. See Kant 1966a: parr. 46 and 47.

15. See especially Rousseau 1762a: 22–23.

16. Kant 1966a: 341.

17. See Kant 1966a: 341.

18. For a concise and interesting discussion of Hegel's critique of Kant's moral philosophy, see Benhabib 1986: 71–84.

19. For a counterexample of the first kind see Hegel 1971: III (*The Phenomenology of Spirit*), p. 322; for one of the second type, see Hegel 1971, II ("On Natural Right"), p. 466.

20. This argument is succinctly expressed in Hegel 1971: XX (*Lectures on the History of Philosophy*), pp. 368–69. See also Hegel 1971: III (*The Phenomenology of Spirit*), pp. 317–19.

21. See the section of *The Phenomenology of Spirit* dedicated to the distinction between law-giving Reason and law-testing Reason, in Hegel 1971: III, pp. 311–23.

22. See Hegel 1971: I, 326.

23. See par. 153 of Hegel's *Philosophy of Right*, Hegel 1971: VII, 303.

24. Hegel 1953: 40.

25. See Hegel 1953: 83.

26. Hegel 1953: 82.

27. See Kiekegaard 1959: II, 218.

28. Kierkegaard 1959: II, 258–59.

29. See Nietzsche 1956: 160–76. See also Nietzsche 1961: 117–20

30. Nietzsche 1956: 188.

31. See Heidegger 1962, par. 53.

BIBLIOGRAPHY

Althusser, Louis. 1972. *Politics and History* (1952). London: New Left Books.

Aristotle. 1962. *The Politics*. Harmondsworth: Penguin.

———. 1976. *The Nicomachean Ethics*. Harmondsworth: Penguin.

Babbitt, Irving. 1919. *Rousseau and Romanticism*. Boston: Houghton Mifflin Co.

Bell, Daniel. 1976. *The Cultural Contradictions of Capitalism*. New York: Basic Books.

———. 1980. *The Winding Passage*. Cambridge, Mass.: ABT.

Bellah, Robert N. 1970. *Beyond Belief. Essays on Religion in a Post-Traditional World*. New York: Harper & Row.

Bellah, Robert N. et al. 1985. *Habits of the Heart: Individualism and Commitment in American Life*. Berkeley: University of California Press.

Benhabib, Seyla. 1986. *Critique, Norm, and Utopia: A Study of the Foundations of Critical Theory*. New York: Columbia University Press.

Berger, Peter. 1979. "Towards a Critique of Modernity." In Berger, P. *Facing up to Modernity*. Harmondsworth: Penguin.

Berger, Peter, Berger, Brigitte and Kellner, Hansfried. 1973. *The Homeless Mind. Modernization and Consciousness*. New York: Random House.

Berlin, Isaiah. 1958. "Two Concepts of Liberty." In Quinton, A. (ed.). 1967. *Political Philosophy*. Oxford: Oxford University Press.

Berman, Marshall. 1972. *The Politics of Authenticity: Radical Individualism and the Emergence of Modern Society*. New York: Athenaum.

Bobbio, Norberto. 1975. "Hegel und die Naturrechtslehre." In Riedel, M. (ed.) 1975: vol. I, pp. 81–108.

Brétonneau, Giselle. 1977. Stoïcisme et Valeurs chèz J. J. Rousseau. Paris: CDU & SEDES.

Burgelin, Pierre. 1952. *La Philosophie de l'Existence de Jean-Jacques Rousseau*. Paris: Presses Universitaires de France.

Casotti, Mario. 1929. *Il 'Moralismo' di Gian-Giacomo Rousseau*. Milan: Università Cattolica del Sacro Cuore, Vol. XV.

Cassirer, Ernst. 1954. *Rousseau, Kant, Goethe*. Princeton: Princeton University Press.

———. 1963. *The Question of Jean-Jacques Rousseau*. Bloomington: Indiana University Press.

Chapman, John W. 1956. *Rousseau—Totalitarian or Liberal?* New York: Columbia University Press.

Charvet, John. 1974. *The Social Problem in the Philosophy of Rousseau*. London: Cambridge University Press.

Cobban, Alfred. 1934. *Rousseau and the Modern State*. London: George Allen & Unwin.

Colletti, Lucio. 1972. *From Rousseau to Lenin*. (1969). London: New Left Books.

Condorcet, Marquis de. 1971. *Esquisse d'un Tableau Historique des Progrès de l'Esprit Humain*. (1773). Paris: Editions Sociales.

Crocker, Lester G. 1963. "Julie ou la Nouvelle Duplicité." In *Annales de la Societé J. J. Rousseau*. 36, pp. 105–52.

———. 1965. "Rousseau et la Voie du Totalitarisme." In *Annales de Philosophie Politique*. 5, pp. 137–52.

———. 1967. "Introduction." In Rousseau, J. J. *The Social Contract and Discourse on the Origin of Inequality*. New York: Simon and Schuster.

———. 1968. *Rousseau's Social Contract: An Interpretative Essay*. Cleveland: Case Western Reserve University Press.

———. 1971. *Jean-Jacques Rousseau. Vol II.: The Prophetic Voice*. New York/London: Macmillan/Collier.

Deleuze, Gilles and Guattari, Félix. 1977. *Anti-Oedipus*. (1972). New York: Viking Press

Della Volpe, Galvano. 1974. *Rousseau e Marx*. Rome: Editori Riuniti.

Derathé, Robert. 1948. *Le Rationalisme de J. J. Rousseau*. Paris: Presses Universitaires de France.

———. 1950. *J. J. Rousseau et la Science Politique de son Temps*. Paris: Presses Universitaires de France.

Derrida, Jacques. 1976. *Of Grammatology* (1967). Baltimore: Johns Hopkins University Press.

———. 1978. *Writing and Difference* (1966). Chicago: University of Chicago Press.

——. 1981. *Positions* (1972). Chicago: University of Chicago Press.

——. 1982. *Margins of Philosophy* (1972). Chicago: University of Chicago Press.

Dewey, John. 1922. *Human Nature and Conduct*. New York: Henry Holt.

Durkheim, Emile. 1919. "La Pédagogie de Rousseau. Plans de Leçons." In *Revue de Métaphysique et Morale*, 26, pp. 153–80.

——. 1933. *The Division of Labor in Society*. New York: Free Press.

——. 1951. *Suicide* (1897). New York: Free Press.

——. 1956. *Education and Sociology* (1922). Glencoe: Free Press.

——. 1961. *Moral Education: A Study in the Theory and Application of the Sociology of Education* (1925). Glencoe: Free Press.

——. 1965. *Montesquieu and Rousseau*. Ann Arbor: University of Michigan Press.

Dworkin, Ronald. 1985. *A Matter of Principle*. Cambridge, Mass.: Harvard University Press.

——. 1986. *Law's Empire*. Cambridge: Harvard University Press.

Ellis, M. B. 1949. *"Julie ou la Nouvelle Heloïse.": A Synthesis of Rousseau's Thought*. Toronto: University of Toronto Press.

Erickson, Erik. 1959. *Identity and the Life-Cycle*. New York: International Universities Press.

——. 1963. *Childhood and Society*. New York: Norton & Co.

Fetscher, Iring. 1968. *Rousseau's Politische Philosophie*. Neuwied/Berlin: Luchterhand.

Feyerabend, Paul K. 1975. *Against Method*. London: New Left Books.

Foucault, Michel. 1975. *Surveiller et punir*. Paris: Gallimard.

———. 1984. *Histoire de la sexualité*, 3 vol. Paris: Gallimard.

Freud, Sigmund. 1914. "On Narcissism: An Introduction." Standard Edition. 1957. London: Hogarth Press. Vol. 14, pp. 67–102.

———. 1923. *The Ego and the Id*. Standard Edition, Vol. 19 reprinted by Norton & Co., New York.

———. 1930. *Civilization and its Discontents*. Standard Edition, Vol. 21. Reprinted by Norton & Co., New York.

Gadamer, Hans-Georg. 1975. *Truth and Method* (1960). New York: Continuum.

Gehlen, Arnold. 1956. *Urmensch und Spätkultur*. Frankfurt.

———. 1957. *Die Seele im Technischen Zeitalter*. Hamburg.

Grimsley, Ronald. 1969. *Jean-Jacques Rousseau: A Study in Self-awareness*. Cardiff: University of Wales Press.

Habermas, Jürgen. 1962. *Strukturwandel der Öffentlichkeit*. Neuwied. Luchterhand.

———. 1975. *Legitimation Crisis* (1973). Boston: Beacon Press.

———. 1979. *Communication and the Evolution of Society*. Boston: Beacon Press.

———. 1981a. *Theorie des kommunikativen Handelns*, 2 vol. Frankfurt: Suhrkamp.

———. 1981b. "Modernity vs. Post-Modernity." In *New German Critique*, 22.

———. 1983a. "Neoconservative Culture Criticism in the United

States and West Germany: An Intellectual Movement in Two Political Cultures." In *Telos*, 56.

———. 1983b. *Moralbewußtsein und kommunikatives Handeln*. Frankfurt: Suhrkamp.

———. 1985. *Der Philosophische Diskurs der Moderne*. Frankfurt: Suhrkamp.

Hall, Gaston H. 1962. "The Concept of Virtue in 'La Nouvelle Heloïse'." In *Yale French Studies*, 28, pp. 20–34.

Hartmann, Heinz. 1964. *Essays in Ego Psychology*. New York: International Universities Press.

Hegel, Georg W. F. 1953. *Reason in History: A General Introduction to the Philosophy of History* (1837). Indianapolis: Bobbs-Merrill.

———. 1971. *Werke in Zwanzig Bänden*. Theorie Werkausgabe. Frankfurt: Suhrkamp.

Heidegger, Martin. 1962. *Being and Time* (1927). New York: Harper & Row.

———. 1973. "Davoser Disputation." Postscript to *Kant und das Problem der Metaphysik*, 1973. Frankfurt: Klostermann.

———. 1978. "Brief über den Humanismus", (1946). In M. Heidegger, *Wegmarken*. Frankfurt, Klostermann, pp. 311–60.

Hobbes, Thomas. 1972. *Leviathan*. (1651). Harmondsworth: Penguin.

Hochschild, Arlie R. 1979. "Emotion Work, Feeling Rules, and Social Structure." In *American Journal of Sociology*, 85, pp. 551–75.

———. 1983. *The Managed Heart: Commercialization of Human Feeling*. Berkeley: University of California Press.

Inhelder, Barbel and Piaget, Jean. 1958. *The Growth of Logical Thinking*. New York: Basic Books.

———. 1964. *The Early Growth of Logic in the Child: Classification and Seriation*. New York: Harper.

Jimack, Peter D. 1960. "La Genèse et la Rédaction de l' 'Emile' de Jean-Jacques Rousseau." In *Studies on Voltaire and the Eighteenth Century*, 13. Geneva: Institut et Musée Voltaire.

Jouvenel, Bertrand de. 1962. "Rousseau the Pessimist Evolutionist." In *Yale French Studies*, 28, pp. 83–96.

Kant, Immanuel. 1951. *The Critique of Judgment* (1790). New York: Hafner.

———. 1960. *Religion within the Limits of Reason Alone* (1793). New York: Harper & Row.

———. 1963. *On History*. Ed. by L. W. Beck. Indianapolis: Bobbs-Merrill.

———. 1964. *Groundwork of the Metaphysics of Morals* (1785). New York: Harper & Row.

———. 1966. *Education* (1803). Ann Arbor: University of Michigan Press.

———. 1966a. *Metaphysik der Sitten* (1797). Hamburg: Meiner Verlag.

———. 1980. *Anthropologie in pragmatischer Hinsicht* (1798). Hamburg: Meiner Verlag.

———. 1983. *Kritik der praktischen Vernunft* (1788). Leipzig: Reclam Verlag.

Kernberg, Otto. 1975. *Borderline Conditions and Pathological Narcissism*. New York: Jason Aronson.

Kierkegaard, Søren. 1959. *Either/Or* (1843), 2 vol. Garden City, New York: Doubleday.

Klukhohn, Clyde. 1958. "Has There Been a Change in American Values in the Last Generation?." In Morison, E. (ed.) *The American Style: Essays in Value and Performance*. New York: Harpers.

Kohlberg, Lawrence. 1964. "Development of Moral Character and Moral Ideology." In Hoffmann, M. and Hoffmann, L. (eds.) *Review of Child Development Research*. New York: Russell Sage Foundation.

———. 1966. "Cognitive Stages and Pre-School Education." In *Human Development*, 9, pp. 5–17.

———. 1969. *Stages in the Development of Moral Thought and Action*. New York: Holt, Rinehart and Winston.

———. 1971. "From Is to Ought: How to Commit the Naturalistic Fallacy and Get Away With It in the Study of Moral Development." In Mischel, T. (ed.) *Cognitive Development and Moral Education*. Cambridge, Mass.: Center for Moral Education.

———. 1981. *Essays on Moral Development*, vol. I. San Francisco: Harper & Row.

Kohut, Heinz. 1971. *The Analysis of the Self*. New York: International Universities Press.

———. 1977. *The Restoration of the Self*. New York: International Universities Press.

Lacan, Jacques. 1977. Écrits: A Selection. (1966). New York: Norton.

———. 1978. *The Four Fundamental Concepts of Psychoanalysis*. New York: Norton.

Lasch, Christopher. 1980. *The Culture of Narcissism* (1979). London: Sphere Books.

———. 1984. *The Minimal Self*. New York: Norton & Co.

Launay, Michel. 1971. *Jean-Jacques Rousseau: Ecrivain Politique.* Grenoble: C.E.L/A.C.E.R.

Levine, Andrew. 1976. *The Politics of Autonomy: A Kantian Reading of Rousseau's 'Social Contract'.* Amherst: University of Massachusetts Press.

Levi-Strauss, Claude. 1973. *Anthropologie Structurale.* Paris: Plon.

Lipset, Seymour M. 1961. "A Changing American Character?." In Lipset, S. M. and Loewenthal, L. *The Sociology of Culture and the Analysis of Social Character: The Work of David Riesman.* Glencoe: Free Press.

Locke, John. 1947. "Some Thoughts Concerning Education" (1692). In Locke, J. *On Politics and Education.* Roslyn, York: Black.

————. *Essay Concerning Human Understanding* (1689). London: Collier.

Lovejoy, Arthur. 1948. "The Supposed Primitivism of Rousseau's 'Discourse on Inequality'." In Lovejoy, A. *Essays in the History of Ideas.* Baltimore: Johns Hopkins University Press.

Lukes, Steven. 1973. *Emile Durkheim: His Life and Work: A Historical and Critical Study.* Harmondsworth: Penguin.

Lyotard, Jean-Francois. 1979. *La Condition Post-Moderne.* Paris: Edition de Minuit.

MacIntyre, Alasdair. 1981. *After Virtue.* Notre Dame: University of Notre Dame Press.

————. 1984. *Is Patriotism a Virtue?* The Lindley Lecture. University of Kansas.

————. 1988. *Whose Justice? Which Rationality?* Notre Dame: University of Notre Dame Press.

————. 1990. *Three Rival Versions of Moral Enquiry*. London: Duckworth.

Manfredi, Gianfranco. 1978. *L'Amore e gli Amori in J. J. Rousseau*. Milan: Mazzotta.

Marx, John. 1980. "The Ideological Construction of Post-Modern Identity Models in Contemporary Cultural Movements." In Robertson, R. and Holzner, B. (eds.) *Identity and Authority: Explorations in the Theory of Society*. Oxford: Basil Blackwell.

Marx, Karl. 1957. *Grundrisse: Foundations of the Critique of Political Economy*. (1859). New York: Random House.

————. 1967. *Writings of the Young Marx on Philosophy and Society*. Ed. by Easton. L. D. and Guddat, K. H. Garden City: Doubleday Anchor.

Masters, Roger D. 1968. *The Political Philosophy of Rousseau*. Princeton: Princeton University Press.

Mauss, Marcel. 1967. *The Gift* (1925). New York: Norton.

Mauzi, Robert. 1959. "La Conversion de Julie dans 'La Nouvelle Heloïse'." In *Annales de la Societé J. J. Rousseau*, 35, pp. 29–38.

Mead, George H. 1972. *Movements of Thought in the Nineteenth Century*. Ed. by Moore, M. H. Chicago: University of Chicago Press.

————. 1974. *Mind, Self and Society* (1934). Chicago: University of Chicago Press.

Menninger, Karl. 1958. *Theory of Psychoanalytic Technique*. New York: Harper & Row.

Merquior, Jose G. 1980. *Rousseau and Weber: Two Studies in the Theory of Legitimacy*. London: Routledge & Kegan Paul.

Mitzman, Arthur. 1969. *The Iron Cage: An Historical Interpretation of Max Weber*. New York: Grosset & Dunlap.

Mornet, Daniel. 1928. "La Nouvelle Heloïse" de Rousseau: Étude et Analyse. Paris: Mellottée.

Mumford, Lewis. 1970. *The Conduct of Life* (1951). New York: Harcourt Brace Jovanovich.

Namer, Gerard. 1978. *Rousseau Sociologue de la Connaissance*. Paris: Anthoropos.

————. 1979. *Le Système Social de Rousseau: De l'Inégalité Economique à l'Inégalité Politique*. Paris: Anthropos.

Nietzsche, Friedrich. 1956. *The Birth of Tragedy* and *The Genealogy of Morals*. Garden City, New York: Doubleday.

————. 1961. *Thus Spoke Zarathustra* (1883). Harmondsworth: Penguin.

Nisbet, Robert A. 1969. *The Quest for Community*. London: Oxford University Press.

Ortega Y Gasset, Jose. 1972. *The Revolt of the Masses* (1930). London: Unwin.

Osmont, Robert. 1953. "Remarques sur la Genèse et la Composition de la 'Nouvelle Heloïse'." In "Annales de la Societé J. J. Rousseau, 33, pp. 93-148.

Parsons, Talcott and White, Winston. 1964. "The Link Between Character and Society." In Parsons, T. *Social Structure and Personality*. Glencoe: Free Press.

Piaget, Jean. 1952a. *The Origins of Intelligence in Children* (1936). New York: International Universities Press.

————. 1952b. *The Language and Thought of the Child*. London: Routledge & Kegan Paul.

————. 1954. *The Construction of Reality in the Child* (1937). New York: Basic Books.

————. 1965. *The Moral Judgment of the Child* (1932) New York: Free Press.

Piaget, Jean and Inhelder, Barbel. 1956. *The Child's Conception of Space* (1948). New York: Humanities Press.

Plattner, Marc F. 1979. *Rousseau's State of Nature*. De Kalb: Northern Illinois University Press.

Rand, Martin. 1959. *Rousseau's Lehre vom Menschen*. Göttingen: Vandenhoeck & Rupert.

Riedel, Manfred (ed.) 1975. *Materialien zu Hegels Rechtsphilosophie*. Frankfurt: Suhrkamp.

Rieff, Philip. 1961. *Freud. The Mind of the Moralist*. Garden City: Doubleday & Co.

————. 1973. *The Triumph of the Therapeutic* (1966). Harmondsworth: Penguin.

————. 1975. *Fellow Teachers*. London: Faber & Faber.

Riesman, David. 1963. *Individualism Reconsidered* (1954). Glencoe: Free Press.

————. 1964. *The Lonely Crowd* (1950). New Haven: Yale University Press.

————. 1980. "Egocentrism: Is the Amerian Character Changing?." In *Encounter*, Sep.–Oct. 1980, pp. 19–28.

Rorty, Richard. 1980. *Philosophy and the Mirror of Nature*. Princeton: Princeton University Press.

————. 1989. *Contingency, Irony, and Solidarity*. Cambridge: Cambridge University Press.

Rousseau, Jean-Jacques. 1755. "Discourse on the Origin and Foundation of Inequality Among Mankind." In Rousseau, J. J. *The Social Contract and the Discourse on the Origin of Inequality.* Ed. by L. G. Crocker. 1967. New York: Simon and Schuster.

———. 1761. *La Nouvelle Heloïse: Julie, or The New Heloise* 1968. University Park: Pennsylvania State University Press.

———. 1762a. *The Social Contract.* In J. J. Rousseau, *The Social Contract and the Discourse on the Origin of Inequality.* Ed. by L. G. Crocker. 1967. New York: Simon and Schuster.

———. 1762b. *Emile.* London: Dent.

———. 1762c. "Lettre à Mgr. De Beaumont, Archeveque de Paris." In J. J. Rousseau, *Du Contrat Social.* Paris: Editions Garnier.

———. 1770. *Confessions.* Harmondsworth: Penguin.

Sartre, Jean-Paul. 1966. *Being and Nothingness* (1943). New York: Washington Square Press.

———. 1966. "L'universel singulier." In J.-P. Sartre *Situations IX—Mélanges,* 1972. Paris: Gallimard.

Schafer, Roy. 1973. "Concepts of Self and Identity and the Experience of Separation—Individuation in Adolescence." In *Psychoanalytic Quarterly,* 42, pp. 42–59.

Schiller, Friedrich. 1971. *Kallias oder über die Schönheit: Uber Anmut und Würde* (1793). Stuttgart: Reclam.

Schluchter, Wolfgang. 1979. "The Paradox of Rationalization." In Roth, G. and Schluchter, W. *Max Weber's Vision of History: Ethics and Methods.* Berkeley: University of California Press.

———. 1981. *The Rise of Western Rationalism: Max Weber's Developmental History.* Berkeley: University of California Press.

Sennett, Richard. 1978. *The Fall of Public Man*. New York: Knopf.

———. 1980. *Authority*. New York: Knopf.

Shklar, Judith. 1969. *Men and Citizens: A Study of Rousseau's Social Theory*. London: Cambridge University Press.

Simmel, Georg. 1950. *The Sociology of Georg Simmel*. Ed. by K. Wolff. New York: Free Press.

———. 1955. *Conflict & The Web of Group-Affiliations*. New York: Free Press.

———. 1987. "Das individuelle Gesetz" (1913). In G. Simmel, *Das individuelle Gesetz: Philosophische Excurse*, edited by M. Landmann. Frankfurt: Suhrkamp.

Smelser, Neil J. 1980. "Vicissitudes of Work and Love in Anglo-American Society." In N. J. Smelser and E. Erikson (eds.), *Themes of Work and Love in Adulthood*. Cambridge, Mass.: Harvard University Press.

Starobinski, Jean. 1971. *Jean-Jacques Rousseau: La Transparence et l'Obstacle*. Paris: Gallimard.

Steinberg, Jules. 1978. *Locke, Rousseau and the Idea of Consent*. Westport, Conn.: Greenwood Press.

Strauss, Leo. 1953. *Natural Right and History*. Chicago: University of Chicago Press.

Strzyz, Klaus. 1981. *Sozialisation und Narzissmus*. Wiesbaden: Akademische Verlaggesellschaft.

Swanson, Guy E. 1980. "A Basis of Authority and Identity in PostIndustrial Society." In Robertson, R. and Holzner,B (eds.) *Identity and Authority: Explorations in the Theory of Society*. Oxford: Basil Blackwell.

Swidler, Ann. 1980. "Love and Adulthood in American Culture." In Smelser, N. J. and Erikson, E (eds.), *Themes of Work and Love in Adulthood*. Cambridge, Mass.: Harvard University Press.

Szasz, Thomas S. 1974. *The Ethics of Psychoanalysis*. New York: Basic Books.

Talmon, Jacob L. 1970. *The Rise of Totalitarian Democracy* (1952). New York: Norton.

Tawney, Richard H. 1980. *Religion and the Rise of Capitalism* (1922). Harmondsworth: Penguin.

Taylor, Charles. 1989. *Sources of the Self: The Making of the Modern Identity*. Cambridge, Mass.: Harvard University Press, pp. 497–99.

Tocqueville, Alexis de. 1969. *Democracy in America* (1850). Garden City: Doubleday Anchor.

Trilling, Lionel. 1971. *Sincerity and Authenticity*. Cambridge, Mass.: Harvard University Press.

Turner, Ralph H. 1976. "The Real Self: From Institution to Impulse." In *American Journal of Sociology*, 81, pp. 989–1016.

Unger, Roberto M. 1975. *Knowledge and Politics*. New York: Free Press.

Vaughan, Charles E (ed.) 1915. *The Political Writings of Jean-Jacques Rousseau*. Cambridge.

———. 1960. *Studies in the History of Political Philosophy Before and After Rousseau*. New York: Russel & Russel.

Waldron, Jeremy. 1989. "Particular Values and Critical Morality," in *California Law Review*, vol. 77, u. 3, pp. 561–89.

Walzer, Michael. 1983. *Spheres of Justice: A Defense of Pluralism and Equality*. New York: Basic Books.

————. 1987. *Interpretation and Social Criticism*. Cambridge, Mass.: Harvard University Press.

————. 1990. "Two Kinds of Universalism." In M. Walzer, *Nation and Universe: The Tanner Lectures on Human Values*. Salt Lake City: University of Utah Press.

Weber, Marianne. 1950. *Max Weber: Ein Lebensbild*. Heidelberg: Schneider.

Weber, Max. 1958. *The Protestant Ethic and the Spirit of Capitalism* (1905). New York: Scribner.

————. 1975. "Religious Rejections of the World and Their Directions" (1915) In Gerth, H. H. and Wright-Mills, C (eds.) *From Max Weber*. New York: Oxford University Press.

————. 1978. *Economy and Society* (1921). Berkeley: University of California Press.

Wittgenstein, Ludwig. 1931. "Bemerkungen über Frazer's 'The Golden Bough'." In *Synthese*, vol. XVII, 1967.

Wolin, Sheldon. 1960. *Politics and Vision: Continuity and Vision in Western Political Thought*. Boston: Little & Brown.

INDEX

Adorno, T. W., 3, 19.
Alexander, 145.
Althusser, L., 159.
Aristotle, 65, 160, 164.
Authenticity: aesthetic and ethical versions of, contrasted, 114–17; and postmodernist view of the self, 24–25; as *idée-force* of contemporary modernity, 24; as "private virtue", 67, 69, 85–86; contrasted with autonomy, 87–90, 104–05; contrasted with intimacy, 90–91; contrasted with intimacy, 90–91; contrasted with sincerity, 86–87. *See also*: Ethic of authenticity.
Autonomy: and "private virtue", 27, 85; as a dimension of ethical rationalization, 122–26; as ideal implicit in Rousseau's notion of "negative education", 69–71; as ideal of artistic activity, 10; as *idée-force* of early modernity, 24; as induced by "negative education", 81–83; as inner–directed-

ness, 11–12, 26; contrasted with authenticity, 87–90, 104–05; from unrecognized inner urges, 24; in Rousseau's moral psychology, 83–85, 113; in the state of nature, 38; repressive autonomy, 98, 102; thesis of the decline of, 3–4, 8–9. *See also*: ethic of autonomy.

Babbit, I., 102, 164.
Baker, R., xii.
Baudelaire, C., 10, 113, 115.
Beaumont, Monsignor de, 161.
Bell, D., x, 3, 7, 9–11, 13, 14, 17, 18, 19, 21, 22, 23, 113, 130, 153, 154.
Bellah, R., 155.
Benhabib, S., 166.
Berger, B., 155.
Berger, P., 155.
Berkeley, G., 63.
Berlin, I., 60–64, 160.
Berman, M., 158, 163.
Bobbio, N., 160.

185